Conquering the Seven Summits of Sales

Conquering the Seven Summits of Sales

From Everest to Every Business, Achieving Peak Performance

SUSAN ERSHLER *and* JOHN WAECHTER

HARPER
BUSINESS

An Imprint of HarperCollinsPublishers

HarperCollins books may be purchased for educational, business, or sales promotional use. For information, please e-mail the Special Markets Department at SPsales@harpercollins.com.

FIRST EDITION

Designed by Jo Anne Metsch

Library of Congress Cataloging-in-Publication Data has been applied for.

ISBN: 978-0-06-228264-4

14 15 16 17 18   OV/RRD   10 9 8 7 6 5 4 3 2 1

*To our parents, Roy and Mary Ellerman, and
Jack and Roenah Waechter; John's wife, Marka Brooke,
and Sue's husband, Phil.*

*Each instilled a belief that anything is possible
and supported us every step of the way!*

ACKNOWLEDGMENTS

We did not reach mountaintops alone, or complete this book alone. Throughout *Conquering the Seven Summits of Sales*, we've emphasized the importance of teamwork in achieving an ambitious goal, and appreciate the work and dedication of the following individuals whose direct involvement was critical in creating this book.

Ilisa Keith, as a collaborator and personal editor, helped shape and polish our prose to a high standard, ensuring that our points were made clearly, consistently, and in a compelling voice. Ilisa is also the principal of KB Communications LLC, a full-service marketing and public relations agency based in Phoenix. Before launching her firm, Ilisa was a senior vice president at Powell Tate in New York City and held senior positions at global public relations agencies, including Golin/Harris Worldwide and Fleishman-Hillard. During this time, she spearheaded the launch of Coleco's Cabbage Patch Kids and developed marketing support programs for such international clients as Smith-Kline Beecham, Richardson Vicks, Chesebrough-Pond's, Inc., Grand Marnier, and the Rado Watch Company. Ilisa began her career as a health/beauty writer for *Mademoiselle* magazine. She has also served as a board member of Women in Communications and is an active member of Phi Beta Kappa and the International Association of Business Communicators.

James Levine and his colleagues at Levine Greenberg Literary Agency helped guide our efforts through the literary industry and were instrumental with feedback and support throughout this process. Jim also worked with Sue on her first book, *Together on Top of the World*. We truly appreciate his passion for the publishing business and his knowledge of the industry.

Thank you to our editor, Colleen Lawrie, and the entire team at HarperCollins, in making this vision a reality. Beyond being an expert editor, Colleen brought critical and creative thinking and a very positive attitude to our partnership. And we sincerely thank Hollis Heimbouch, publisher at Harper Business; Joanna Pinsker, our publicity manager; and Christine Choe, our marketing professional.

John and Sue had great fortune to have worked with, and continue to work with, many great mentors, coworkers, direct reports, clients, and business partners. Their relationships with these people have yielded lifelong friendships and provided the many lessons and stories recounted in this book. While there are far too many to name, we want to mention the following people for their mentorship, guidance, partnership, and inspiration to get the job done!

- *Sue's speaker bureau partners*, who have provided friendship and expertise for over a decade in supporting Sue's professional speaking career.

- *Greg Wilson*: Everest mountain guide (2001) and friend, who, with Phil, guided our 2001 Everest expedition and was instrumental in that team's success. Greg also summited Mount Everest as part of the 1991 American North Face Expedition, and is now a middle school teacher in Hailey, Idaho.

- *Our Everest Sherpas*, notably our lead Sherpa, Ang Passang, and Sherpas Dorjee Lama and Danuru Sherpa. The many Sherpa climbers who routinely support Himalayan expeditions are critical to the safety and success of all who venture onto the world's highest mountains.

- *John Whetzell*, CEO of Northland Communications Corporation: client, friend, boss, and the one who introduced Sue and Phil!

- *Walt Yeager*, former sales manager at GTE (now Verizon): boss, mentor, friend, and person responsible for managing John and Sue at the same time!

- *Jay Tyler*, former district sales manager, Xerox: boss, mentor, and friend who taught John how to manage "Attitude and Activities"!

- *Andy Lufkin*, partner and portfolio manager, Delafield Hambrecht, Inc.: lifelong friend, business partner, and climbing partner. Two to go!

- And finally to our wonderful community of friends and family who have wholeheartedly supported our endeavors and made our lives richer along the way. Most notably, a special thanks to Phil Ershler, Sue's husband, our mountain guide and trusted leader throughout our Seven Summits journey, for his inspiration and guidance in helping us achieve our Seven Summits dream. Phil first achieved this feat in 1989 and then again in 2002, this time with Sue at his side. Phil is renowned internationally for his consummate skills as a mountaineer, guide, and climbing instructor. He was the first American to climb the north face of Mount Everest in 1984 and has summited Mount Rainier well over 400 times. Climbing is Phil's passion, avocation, and vocation. As cofounder of International Mountain Guides, LLC, a worldwide guiding company, he too has applied lessons from the mountains to success in business.

Thank you.

CONTENTS

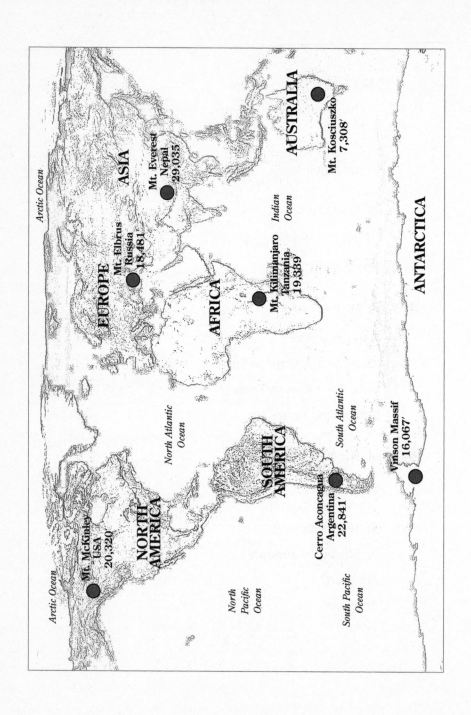

INTRODUCTION

On May 25, 2001, at 3:00 a.m., we slowly approached the Balcony on the southeast ridge of Mount Everest, battling the frigid fifty-mile-per-hour winds and needles of snow. Both of us had reached the pinnacle of our profession as sales executives and entrepreneurs. Yet here we were, risking our lives and everything we had worked so hard to attain. Exhausted, we lifted our bodies onto the Balcony's narrow ledge, removed our oxygen masks, and, huddling together, asked ourselves, "Why are we trying to climb this 29,035-foot mountain?"

The answer was a simple one. We cherished the deep satisfaction that only comes from attaining a seemingly impossible goal through focus, determination, and perseverance. For us, Everest represented the very pinnacle of achievement and the capstone of our journey to join the elite group of climbers who have conquered the Seven Summits, the highest peaks on each of the seven continents.

Both of us would ultimately achieve this goal, applying the same skills and strategies that helped us climb the corporate ladder and become top sales performers. In the years that followed, we would draw upon our Seven Summits experiences to lead sales organizations and to launch and grow businesses. We would also share these experiences when conducting sales keynotes and presentations for major corporations around the world, inspiring sales and business professionals to overcome their perceived limitations and achieve their own visions of personal and professional success.

As longtime friends, fellow climbers, and business professionals, we shared a unique perspective about the parallels between success in sales and on the mountain. One morning about two years ago, we were having coffee and sharing some recent speaking experiences. Invariably audience members would ask us questions that revolved around two key themes: "Do you have to be a born salesperson or can anyone learn to achieve sales success?" and "How does someone take on a huge challenge like climbing Everest and then go about achieving it?"

As we thought about it, we reached the conclusion that both questions could be answered in the same way. We both firmly believe that achievement in any sphere of life is an acquired skill. It's a strategic approach to problem solving that can be learned and perfected over time. In that moment, we knew that we had the basis for an instructive and entertaining "how-to" book on sales, one that would allow us to share our experiences and apply the metaphors of mountain climbing to success in the business world.

We began by conducting some competitive research. After reading dozens of sales books, we concluded that we could bring a fresh new perspective to a heavily traveled subject. We spoke to hundreds of businesspeople and solicited their feedback and suggestions. We soon realized that the lessons we'd learned and the strategies we'd honed in business and mountain climbing would be beneficial not only to salespeople, but to a much broader audience as well.

According to the U.S. Bureau of Labor Statistics, one in nine Americans holds a position in sales. In today's competitive marketplace, salespeople and leaders need a book like ours as never before. In recent years, sales expectations and revenue goals have increased, even though many companies have been forced to cut back sharply on their training programs. Information overload is rampant, as mobile technologies and social networking create new distractions that can impede success. We resolved that our book would help salespeople and leaders navigate these obstacles and excel at what really counts: generating revenue and forging productive long-term customer relationships.

But this tells only part of the story. Virtually every business professional is expected to develop client relationships, produce revenue opportunities, and help their company compete successfully in the marketplace. So developing sales skills is essential for anyone who hopes to climb the corporate ladder or start their own business. Yet few companies offer sales training to their marketing, finance, customer support, operations, and other customer-facing organizations. We decided that our book would fill this gap while providing fresh perspectives on best-practice selling and productivity techniques.

Now, two years after that fateful cup of coffee, you can see the results of our literary journey here, in the pages of *Conquering the Seven Summits of Sales.*

The book is organized into three sections, each featuring chapters describing our experiences climbing the Seven Summits and illustrating key elements of the selling process. We've also provided numerous worksheets that will help you put these lessons into practice. We hope you will walk away from this book newly energized, inspired, and equipped with the basic and advanced selling skills you need to achieve your own vision of high achievement.

—Susan Ershler and John Waechter

PART I

PROJECT

Mount Everest—South Col to the Summit. *(Greg Vernovage)*

1

COMMIT TO THE SUMMIT

PROJECT: Every success begins with an ambitious and clearly articulated vision.

If you want to be happy, set a goal that commands your thoughts, liberates your energy, and inspires your hopes.
—Andrew Carnegie, founder of Carnegie Steel Company

Mount Everest is located in the Himalayan Range on the border between Nepal and Tibet in Asia. At 29,035 feet, Everest is the tallest mountain on Earth and the most dangerous of the Seven Summits to climb. More than 250 climbers have lost their lives there.

It was May 24, 2001. After sixty-three days of climbing Mount Everest, Sue and John had just one day left to reach the summit. It was late in the climbing season, the weather was looking ominous, and their goal of reaching the top of the world and completing their Seven Summits quest would come down to one last push.

Human bodies aren't designed to operate efficiently at extreme altitudes. Above 24,600 feet, sleeping becomes difficult, digesting food is almost impossible, and climbers face an increased risk of high-altitude pulmonary edema (HAPE) and high-altitude cerebral edema (HACE). These conditions, caused by low oxygen, can often prove fatal. Contending with headaches, nausea, and persistent fatigue, climbers quickly exhaust their energy stores and begin to rapidly lose weight.

Sue and John were now at 26,000 feet, an altitude known as the Death Zone. At this elevation, virtually every human— unless they receive supplementary oxygen—will begin to experience a rapid deterioration of bodily functions that leads inexorably to loss of consciousness and, eventually, death. On the evening before their final 3,000-foot push to the summit, John and Sue huddled anxiously in their tents against the freezing temperatures and howling wind. The climb awaiting them would be the most difficult of their lives. Would they be able to summon the drive and energy they would need to succeed?

The storm that had arrived the day before was building in strength when they dragged themselves from their tents at 11:00 P.M. to survey the conditions and make final preparations. After forcing themselves to take a few sips of water, they began to climb. It was almost midnight and pitch-black. The jet stream had moved in like a freight train, bringing heavy winds that drove needles of snow into their faces. They could barely see each other as they climbed into the darkness.

Sue struggled as she ascended a series of steps that had clearly been carved into the icy mountain for climbers with legs much longer than her own. It was like climbing a staircase made of chairs. Slowly, painfully, she trudged on, following the pale circle of light cast by her headlamp on the snow.

Her muscles were already sore from months of climbing and years of training. Her pack felt heavier and her headlamp cord froze where it snaked against her neck. The vent in her oxygen mask, which allowed her exhaled breath to escape so she wouldn't suffocate, kept freezing over, too. Every few steps, she had to stop to break the ice. And no matter how she adjusted the ascender in her safety harness, it kept banging painfully against her knee. Her fingers were stinging and she couldn't feel her toes. She began flexing them, hoping to prevent frostbite from setting in. To keep herself going, she chanted the three mantras she'd written in her journal:

You have the ability; now believe, believe, believe.

Olympic athletes perform through the pain. So can you.

Pain is temporary, push through the pain.

Somewhere up ahead, John too was facing the harsh realities of climbing in the Death Zone. The thin air had affected his ability to think clearly, a condition known as hypoxia that results from diminished oxygen levels to the brain. This lightheadedness had caused John to vacillate when determining which gloves to wear from High Camp to the summit. Warm down mittens would provide maximum protection against the harsh elements, but they would restrict the dexterity needed to handle the fixed ropes and devices required to climb. Ultimately he had chosen thin gloves that provided little protection against the frigid wind and subzero temperatures. Now, he was losing feeling in his fingers despite his repeated attempts to keep the circulation flowing. Ignoring the numbness and stinging pain, John continued climbing. As he approached 27,600 feet—only approximately 1,400 feet from the summit—the wind and snow began to batter his face harder than ever and his progress slowed. He became increasingly certain that the mountain was not going to be climbable that day. Disappointment began to dampen his spirits.

After hours of climbing, Sue and John came together for a break with the one other team that was on the upper mountain that night—an American team striving to get the first blind climber to the top of the world. This team was also diminished, so the two teams discussed their plans and agreed to watch out for one another as they climbed the next leg.

Although climbers work as a team, each is alone when it comes to marshaling the strength and endurance needed to overcome the challenges of a serious climb. During the past sixty-three days of their climb, Sue and John had many long hours to think about their motivation and push down the voices inside their heads saying things like "What in the world are you doing up here? You're not a professional mountain climber. Why put yourself through this kind of pain?"

Scaling a Quota

Two months earlier, before attacking the perils of Everest, Sue and John had faced equally daunting challenges in their business careers. Sue was at US West (now CenturyLink), a Fortune 500 telecommunications service provider, where she led the sales organization responsible for the firm's largest Internet service provider (ISP) accounts. How, she wondered, would they overcome fierce competition, rapid market changes, and limited resources to achieve the dramatic increase in their revenue objectives—from $250 million to $300 million—that had just been mandated by senior management?

John was mulling over the future of Waechter Lufkin, LLC, the boutique investment banking firm he had cofounded four years earlier with his friend and fellow climber Andy Lufkin. The company, which specialized in providing guidance and venture capital to start-up technology companies, had enjoyed enormous success throughout the technology boom of the late 1990s. Then, just prior to the Everest expedition, the bubble burst, plunging the country into recession. John would now have to define a new vision and business strategy to maintain the growth the company had enjoyed until then. However, with Everest looming, this was a challenge that would have to wait until he returned from the mountain.

As sales professionals, we're accustomed to high pressure and seemingly unreasonable expectations. We're always being challenged to do more with less. We're expected to find new clients, service existing ones, and stay current with industry trends while meeting strict deadlines. Somehow, through all this, we must also find time to have a personal life. And if you're in a management role, as we were, you have the added responsibility of successfully building and leading a team.

Have you ever felt stymied while chasing a dream? Felt like you've only just started, yet the obstacles you're encountering already seem overwhelming? "This is too difficult," you tell yourself. "How will I ever make it happen?"

We've been there too. But through experience, we've learned that anyone can overcome seemingly insurmountable obstacles and achieve their personal vision of success.

Project. Prepare. Persevere

The act of climbing a mountain has long captured the human imagination as a metaphor for meeting life's challenges. On the mountain, we must overcome harsh weather and physical barriers to reach the summit. In business, sales professionals must overcome constant rejection and scarce resources to fulfill their quotas and earn financial rewards.

We're proud to count ourselves among the elite climbers who have ascended the Seven Summits, the highest mountains on each of the seven continents. In sales too there are Seven Summits that every top performer must conquer, one for each chapter of this book.

Your journey through our Seven Summits of Sales will proceed through three distinct phases that we refer to as **Project. Prepare. Persevere**. This is a methodology for achieving both short- and long-term goals that will help you develop the essential skills and attitudes common to Everest summiteers and top sales performers alike. This book is divided into three parts, one for each phase.

In our first two chapters, we'll discuss *projecting* your vision, setting goals, and creating action plans. In chapters 3 to 6, we'll examine the nuts and bolts of *preparing* to be successful by learning about your company, products, and services, and by acquiring the in-depth market knowledge and industry expertise you'll need to perform at the elite level. We'll also consider how to leverage this knowledge so you can navigate effectively through the sale process.

We'll conclude the book in chapter 7, where we'll explore the keystone trait that every top performer possesses: *perseverance*. We'll show you that perseverance is something that can be learned and perfected, like any other skill. And we'll provide practical methods you can use to ignite your passion and overcome any obstacle in your path to success.

For more than eight years, we fully committed ourselves to achieving our vision of climbing the Seven Summits. We trained year-round and spent all of our annual vacations pursuing this goal with single-minded determination. Along the way, our climbing experiences proved to be a rich source of inspiration, bringing us new skills and perspectives that we could leverage to achieve success in every aspect of our lives. Throughout this book, we'll illustrate these principles with anecdotes from our business and climbing careers and show you how to apply them in attaining your own vision of personal and professional success.

Project Your Future—CLIMB

It all begins with a well-defined vision and a set of clearly defined goals. The CLIMB system we developed on our journey to becoming top performers will provide you with a structured approach to goal setting that is both disciplined and focused.

Let's take a look at a leading executive who used our CLIMB principles to achieve remarkable success in a rapidly changing industry. Marka Jenkins, CEO of Metropolitan Travel, was recognized nationwide as one of the top executives in the travel industry. Prior to her stewardship, Metropolitan Travel enjoyed considerable success by delivering exemplary customer service and innovations in travel man-

C	Concise	Your goals must be specific, quantifiable, actionable, and support your vision.
L	Levelheaded	Your vision *and* goals must be realistic and attainable based on your current skills and level of professional development.
I	Integrated	Your goals must be related, relevant, and integrated with your vision.
M	Measurable	You must hold yourself accountable by using objective metrics to track your progress against goals. You must "measure the mountain."
B	Big	Being realistic doesn't mean thinking small. Be bold and ambitious in projecting your future. Think Big!

agement consulting to an impressive roster of corporate clients under the leadership of her business partner, and chairman, Jeff Schoenfeld.

Then the Internet arrived and hit the travel industry hard. Airlines began reducing their commissions to travel agencies, eroding their core revenue streams, and making it increasingly difficult for the travel industry to operate profitably. More worrisome, travel agencies were now facing new competition from companies planning to offer ticketing and reservation systems directly to customers through the Internet. If this took hold, travel agencies like Metropolitan Travel faced the very real threat that the foundation for their service-based business was in serious jeopardy.

This message of impending change was brought home with a vengeance when Marka attended a speech given by Bill Gates to alumni at his high school alma mater, the Lakeside School. His words were blunt and to the point. If you don't have a business vision that includes the Internet, your company won't survive the coming decade. It was a wake-up call for Marka. She started to educate herself about online business models and soon set a new strategic course for their company, one that accounted for the coming marketplace changes while retaining the values that Jeff established to set Metropolitan Travel apart from the competition.

They began with a new vision: to become the intelligent choice for corporate travel management by delivering exceptional customer service along with innovative Internet-based tools for travel management. As part of the branding overhaul, the company would change its tag line to "Self-service when you want it; full service when you need it!"

Marka relied on the principles of the CLIMB system to reposition their company for success in a rapidly changing marketplace. Let's see how our CLIMB methodology helped Marka achieve her vision and goals:

- *Concise*: Marka's vision was to build an Internet-based reservation system that would meet the following criteria:
  - It would innovate by enforcing company travel policies.
  - It would be so easy to use, it would encourage self-service.
  - It would retain a full-service component while providing convenient online access to booking information.

- *Levelheaded*: Metropolitan Travel possessed deep operational knowledge about the inner workings of the various airline ticketing and reservation systems, which gave the firm a distinct advantage over competitors whose expertise was primarily in software development. The company made sure to recruit a talented team of developers able to apply this subject matter expertise when developing the company's new software.

- *Integrated*: To survive in the new environment, Metropolitan Travel would need to integrate its new self-service systems with its proven methods for delivering high-quality, personal service.

- *Measurable*: Marka and her team took a comprehensive and disciplined approach to project management, tracking the development process and deliverables closely and ensuring they were on time and within budget. Then, when the software was deployed, they measured the extent to which clients were utilizing the self-service capabilities by comparing the number of bookings made online versus offline and the level of satisfaction clients expressed about each method.

- **Big**: Marka's goal to develop a new system was extremely ambitious for a moderately sized company like Metropolitan Travel, especially since it placed the company in direct competition with industry giants like Microsoft, American Express, and Galileo. However, they felt confident that the firm's domain expertise would give them an edge, resulting in a system that offered a superior user experience.

Marka had always believed that Metropolitan Travel's new software would be attractive to other similarly sized travel companies. So, a year later, when development was complete, she formed a new company, HighWire, to market the booking software, which was now known as Travelport. However, she had not fully appreciated the appeal the new software would have for large corporations until 2001, when Microsoft Corporation selected Travelport as its internal travel booking system. Then, just six months later, Galileo, now owned by Cendant Corporation, acquired HighWire outright after failing to deliver the booking system it had been developing for its own network of travel agent clients. Thinking big had paid off handsomely.

Thanks to Marka's vision and the CLIMB methodology, her company weathered the subsequent contraction of the industry, which saw more than five hundred travel agencies shut their doors between 2000 and 2002.

Let's now take a closer look at our CLIMB system and consider how it enabled Sue and John to become top performers in sales and how you can apply these same methods to achieve your own vision and goals.

Be Concise: Write Down Your Summit Goals

Your goals must be so specific and quantifiable that you can write them down easily. In 2001, Sue's goals were 29,035 feet and $300 million. The first is the height of Mount Everest. The second was her sales team's revenue objective for that year. She posted these goals on yellow sticky notes on her computers at home and at work.

John's goals were equally tangible and concrete. The first was two, the number of mountains he had left to climb to achieve his Seven Summits vision. The second was 100 percent, the revenue growth he was determined to achieve for Waechter Lufkin following the collapse of the technology sector. Although he had not yet fully developed a new strategic vision for the firm, John knew that it was essential to begin by setting a specific growth target. He felt confident that his company could not only survive the uncertain times but also could ultimately thrive by focusing on the best technology companies in the Pacific Northwest and by expanding the firm's focus to additional industry sectors. In time, he would achieve both of these goals and many more.

Are you ready to take the first step toward your *own* summit of achievement? If so, take out two blank three-by-five-inch cards. Stop and think for a moment. What would be the greatest personal achievement you could possibly imagine for yourself? What would be the greatest professional achievement? Write both of them down on one of the cards. This is your **Vision Card**.

Apple cofounder Steve Jobs once said, "Death is the destination we all share. No one has ever escaped it. Live each day as if it was your last. Our time is limited, so don't waste it." We couldn't agree more. Life is short and time is ticking. So think big and get ready to live your dream.

Now, consider the goals you must achieve on your way to fulfilling the dreams on your Vision Card. Make sure they are as simple and concrete as possible. One word, one number, or a short phrase is perfect. Write them down on the second card. This is your Summit Card.

On your third card, write down the key elements of the campaign you will wage to achieve your goals. This is your Activities Card. Below, you'll find an example of what Sue wrote on her Vision, Summit, and Activities cards.

The next step is the most important one of all. If you're really serious about turning your dreams and goals into reality, do what every top athlete in the world does. Burn them into your mind. Look at your Vision and Summit cards several times every day until you nail them.

VISION CARD

I will:

Lead my team to top performance.

Achieve President's Club.

Be promoted to VP of sales.

Stand on the summit of Everest.

SUMMIT CARD

I will:

Blow away my $300 million goal.

Achieve my stretch goal of $400 million.

Complete a hundred hikes (2,000-vertical -foot gain each) within twelve months.

ACTIVITIES CARD

I will:

Increase my client face time.

Decrease my administrative task load.

Build stronger relationships with my client executives.

Focus upon and create detailed account plans for the top ten clients in our territory.

Educate our clients about our value proposition.

Focus on our fastest-growing vertical markets.

Stay current on our product and services.

After a short break, Sue and John resumed their Everest climb, buoyed by the companionship of the other climbing team. Finally, hours later, they reached the Balcony, an ice ledge about 1,400 feet from the summit, where they stopped to change their oxygen bottles. The storm had worsened to whiteout conditions. They could see lightning strikes on the surrounding mountains. The frigid wind seemed strong enough to send them tumbling off the ledge if they weren't careful. Soon, everyone on the team was covered with a layer of ice, shivering in the extreme cold.

When faced with such dangerous conditions and the uncertainty they bring, guides ask themselves one key question: "Is it safe for the team to continue or should we turn back?" Sue watched as her husband, Phil, and their friend Greg Wilson, who were jointly guiding the climb, huddled together discussing their options. At first, when Phil informed Greg he was having trouble with his vision, Greg felt that the safest course would be for the entire team to turn back. Phil disagreed. "You and John are still strong," he told Greg. "Go for another half hour and make a decision then."

Phil trudged over to Sue, shouting to be heard over the wind. "It's too dangerous for us to go any farther," he said. "I'm going to take you down. But Greg and John are going to continue for a little longer. Can you live with that?" Sue's first reaction was relief. They were alive and together. That's all that mattered. She nodded her agreement, and they began their descent.

Two hours later, Sue noticed something strange. Phil—who normally moved with great precision—kept stumbling and losing his balance. This grew steadily worse until he finally turned to her and asked, "Sue, is there something in my eyes?"

When she looked at him, what she saw shocked her. Icicles were hanging from his eyebrows and lashes. The skin under his eyes was white and frozen. Worse, his corneas had frozen over and turned his irises from their customary brown to a purplish hue. This was causing a significant loss of vision, which he described as looking through wax paper. Fortunately the effects were temporary and his vision returned to normal a few days later. But if they hadn't turned around when they did, Phil might have lost his vision entirely or suffered a fatal accident in a place that was already incredibly risky to traverse, even for someone with perfectly clear vision. They had made the right decision, not just for Sue's safety but, in the end, for Phil's too.

John and Greg collected their thoughts, discussed their strategy, and with renewed focus and determination assembled their gear and affixed their oxygen masks. Then they began heading upward through the darkness and blinding snow on their way to the summit.

Sue's Everest vision deferred. *(Charlie Peck)*

Levelheaded: Charting Realistic Goals Begins with Self-Assessment

Few salespeople aim just to meet a quota and nothing more. Most of us dream of being at the top of our field. But top performers do much more than dream. They develop a series of realistic goals that will propel them from where they are now to where they want to be. Next, they continue raising the bar, setting increasingly ambitious goals for themselves until they achieve their ultimate vision of success. Then they start the process all over again. In every case, this process begins with a realistic self-assessment of their current skills and capabilities.

Self-assessment can be a tricky business. We discovered this when—in the early stages of planning our Seven Summits campaign—Phil turned to us and said, "You don't even know if you can physically go that high." What did that mean? Of *course* we could go high! We worked out every day. We had climbed smaller mountains. We would work *really, really* hard!

Some people, Phil explained, could not physically tolerate the low oxygen and harsh conditions found at the very highest mountain peaks. No matter how hard they worked, they would never survive such a climb. Fortunately it turned out we were among the lucky ones. Our bodies were able to tolerate extreme altitudes.

In business too some people may feel that their dreams are beyond their capabilities. They imagine insurmountable obstacles and decide that they simply can't "go high" in their sales careers. But in this case there's no question of biology. *Anyone* can become a top performer. You—yes, you!—can become the number one salesperson in your organization.

Let's start your plan for success with a self-assessment. Take a moment now to reflect on three basic questions:

1. What is preventing you from achieving your business goals?

2. What barriers are standing between you and your dreams?

3. What goals must you achieve to overcome them?

As you reflect, you may realize that some of the obstacles standing between you and your business goals have very little to do with business. Consider every aspect of your life that might be preventing you from becoming a top performer:

- Do I fully understand my company's products and services?

- Do I fully grasp my competitor's strengths and weaknesses?

- Do I truly give my best effort every day and tackle the most challenging tasks first?

- Am I getting enough sleep?

- Am I exercising regularly and rigorously?

- Am I maintaining a healthy and balanced diet?

- Am I maintaining my most important personal relationships?

No doubt you can come up with additional examples. Write all of them down. Then, after you finish reading the rest of this chapter, revisit them and make sure your list is both accurate and complete. Congratulations! You now have a firm basis for creating an "obstacle elimination plan"!

Successful salespeople achieve their vision by pursuing a series of realistic goals that they attain one by one in exactly the same way we climb mountains: one step after the next. But, the number of steps we must take depends on where we start on our journey.

Take a moment now to consider three very different individuals: Bill, Ann, and Cathy. Each has a vision of becoming number one. All three are fully capable of achieving this. But to get there, they need realistic plans that reflect their experience, past performance, and stage of professional development. These plans must address the unique sequence of goals each of them must fulfill to become number one. **Effective plans are realistic and achievable.**

Bill, Ann, and Cathy represent broad classes of experience and past performance. (Ask yourself: which one am I?) All three are capable of becoming number one. But is this a realistic short-term goal?

Bill is just getting started. And, while he may impress some by trumpeting his lofty ambitions, he needs to focus on acquiring the sales skills and tools he'll need to prospect and close business. Bill's first summit goal should be to emerge as the best trainee in the group. That's not only a realistic first goal but it also sets him up for the next summit and the one after, which will ultimately lead him to his number one spot.

In our profession, statistically most salespeople are like Ann. Ann

Salesperson	Goal	Experience Level	Past Performance	Realistic?	First Summit Goal
Bill	#1	New employee. In training. No territory as-signed.	None	No	Complete training as the top trainee.
Ann	#1	Multiple years.	Average. Kept her job but never broke into the top 25%.	Doubtful	Break into the top 25% and become a consistent per-former.
Cathy	#1	Multiple years.	Above average. Has performed consistently in the top 25%.	Yes!	Go for it!

Three salespeople, same goal. Which ones are realistic?

keeps her job because she satisfies her sales quota most of the time. She doesn't win prizes and is seldom recognized at sales meetings. She is just getting by.

Ann *could* become number one. But such a dramatic turnaround would probably be the result of luck rather than planning. A beautiful bluebird could fly through her open window and land on her prospect list. We all love unexpected wins like these. But we certainly shouldn't plan on them!

A more viable goal for Ann is to increase her level of activity and break into the top 10 to 25 percent group. This goal is realistic, since Ann has several years of experience and clearly understands her company and its products and services. (We'll give you the tools you need to acquire this knowledge in subsequent chapters. We'll also cover prospecting and qualifying.)

Ann clearly knows what she's doing. She just isn't doing enough. She needs a plan with a sequence of realistic and quantifiable mini-goals:

- She will make five to ten additional prospecting calls every day.

- She will increase her weekly face-to-face meetings with clients by 10 percent.

- She will contact every prospect at least once a week to assess where they are in the sales cycle.

- She will allocate one additional hour each day to learning more about the products offered by her company and its competitors.

- She will meet with her managers every week to avail herself of their expertise and experience and to secure their help in keeping her first summit goal front and center.

Notice that each of Ann's minigoals includes a realistic metric. A goal of making a hundred additional prospecting calls each day is unrealistic. By starting slowly and staying on track, Ann will make it to the top.

Cathy is among the top sales performers at her company. Year after year, she's proven that she possesses the sales skills and consistency to become number one. She knows how to prospect, qualify, close business, and maintain customer relationships. Yet the top spot has eluded her so far. What's holding her back?

Cathy's problem is one of vision. She's always marveled at the recognition and rewards afforded top performers. She simply can't picture herself among them. So she has never invested the necessary time and effort to become number one.

Every climber will tell you that the last thousand feet to the summit are the toughest. Cathy's plan must begin with a deeply felt vision. She needs to leave her comfort zone and envision herself on top. That will give her the motivation she needs to finish her climb.

Cathy's plan must reflect her advanced level of professional development. She should increase the number of prospecting calls she makes each day and follow up more frequently with the most qualified candidates. She should look for ways to expand her market opportunity by educating herself about the fastest growing sectors within her territory. She should maintain contact with her existing clients by setting up meetings to share her expertise and stay abreast of their needs. When you're as tenured and accomplished as Cathy, you should be setting only the highest standards for yourself and your performance. And then you should commit to them every day by proclaiming, "I will increase my daily activities, I will achieve my weekly goals, I will become the top-performing salesperson in my company this year!"

Bill, Ann, and Cathy have very different plans. All of them are realistic and achievable. But none of them can be accomplished without effort. Every salesperson experiences setbacks along the way. You may start to believe that your goals are beyond your reach. But if you push on, you'll discover that this isn't so. You'll simply be passing through what we call the Discomfort Zone.

On the mountain, every climber is tired, cold, and contending with extreme discomfort as they move from one camp to the next. But, except for those few of us who are physically unable to go high, we are not facing a true barrier. Our plan to reach the summit is both realistic and achievable.

Bill can't become number one in the near term because he doesn't have a territory. That is a real barrier. Other barriers are illusory. When Ann fails to identify new opportunities after making a long series of prospecting calls, she may tell herself that her goal is unrealistic. She's wrong. She's just climbing her way through the Discomfort Zone.

With realistic goals and the right plan, you too can achieve your vision. Without a plan, disaster can strike without warning, as Sue learned firsthand during her first sales job.

Sue says: When I was thirty years old and new to the technology field, a former boss, Walt, invited me to join a Fortune 500 technology firm and work for him as a major account manager. I was thrilled. Up to that point, I had always worked in operations. Now I would hold a high-level sales position, one that offered unlimited earning potential. It was the job of my dreams.

When I arrived, I was a typical sales newbie, with lots of enthusiasm and drive. Unfortunately, I lacked the vision, goals, planning skills, sales experience, and training that would have enabled me to harness this energy and put it to good use. When it came to sales, I was utterly clueless.

One day I called on the second largest law firm in Seattle to present a telephone system I hoped would lead to a sale. The meeting was very pleasant. I had a nice chat with the client. But the meeting produced absolutely nothing in the way of next steps.

Afterward I drove back to the office with one of my firm's top salespeople. Along the way, he turned to me and asked, "How close are you to fulfilling your $1 million objective?" After a short pause, I admitted that I didn't know. He looked at me in disbelief. "You won't last very long in sales if you don't always know exactly where you stand in meeting your quota," he said sternly. "We're nearing the end of the year. When you get back to the office, you'd better find out."

A few days later, Walt took me out for coffee. I usually enjoyed spending time with my friend and mentor. But this time, the atmosphere felt strained. Walt couldn't bring himself to look me in the eye. He kept staring down at his coffee cup.

Finally, he said, "Sue, there's going to be a major reorganization soon. The leadership team feels it would be better for the company—and for you especially—if you were moved to a department that sells lower cost systems requiring less technical knowledge and selling experience." Walt had done everything he could to help me thrive in my major account role, but he could no longer protect me. Hurt and embarrassed, I decided to quit. That night, I tossed and turned, unable to sleep.

By the next morning, however, I found a new level of resolve. I would fight to save my position. I began by drawing on a great piece of advice Walt had once given me. "Focus, become an expert in one industry."

I returned to the office with a new vision. I would become an expert in selling to law firms. I would learn to speak their language and understand their needs, their competitors, and their industry challenges. I would plan and map out every call in advance. I would drive results and win recognition as a top performer.

I knew that I would have to work extremely hard to make up for my inexperience. I might not yet possess the skills needed to out-sell the top sales performers. But I could certainly outwork them.

After a year of focusing on my vision and outworking my peers, I closed one of the largest contracts in my company's history and achieved 190 percent of my revenue objective. By all accounts, the leadership team was shocked by my unexpected success. Soon afterward, I was restored to my major account manager position.

Suddenly I was no longer being ignored in the office. I had earned respect. Management began asking for my opinions about the company's products and marketplace challenges. I started winning promotions and climbing the corporate ladder. Success was sweet. I had committed myself to becoming a top performer. I would become the best that I could possibly be.

Sue's first experiences in sales are hardly unique. Most of us fail before we succeed. But the principles of early success are straightforward and easily grasped. Here are four key lessons:

- Have a vision and focus.

- Become an expert in one thing and do it perfectly.

- Work extra hard to offset your inexperience.

- Drive results. This is the great "equalizer." If you drive results, you will be valued and respected by your colleagues and leadership team.

Integrated: Vision Drives Activity

When Sue decided to climb Everest, her biggest challenge was meeting the demands of her career in sales leadership while making time for the arduous, yearlong training regimen that would prepare her physically and mentally to reach the summit.

In sales, we're constantly bombarded with demands for our time. There are reports to fill out, hundreds of e-mails to answer, trade and news magazines to read, and products to learn about. There's so much going on that information overload is a very real possibility.

The key is to jettison everything that does not lead directly to fulfilling your vision. As a sales leader, Sue helped her team focus exclusively on activities that would help them reach their revenue objective. This included securing support staff to off-load administrative tasks, answering e-mails at the end of the day, and relentlessly tracking their "to do" lists to ensure that they were all focusing on prospecting, calling on clients, and working the sales cycle. When vision drives activity, your priorities quickly fall into place.

Sue and John brought the same approach to their preparations for Everest. They learned early on that, in climbing, the best training is to "do what you're going to do": to practice their climbing skills in a setting that is as close to the one they will encounter later during an expedition. They called this Specificity of Activity. For Sue, this meant climbing at a high altitude on snow and ice with a weighted pack on her back. This is not practical when you live and work at sea level. Sue needed a more realistic plan. But if you commit to a vision, you can always find a way. As she recalls, "During my lunch hours, I would hurry to the restroom, change into my gym clothes, and don a pack filled with weights and kitty litter. Then I would enter the lobby stairwell of my thirty-two-story office building and climb up and down six or seven times as fast as possible. After finishing, I'd change back into my work clothes and eat lunch at my desk. Without my vision, I would never have found the motivation to repeat this exercise every day for a solid year."

Specificity of Activity applies in sales too. Top performers excel at face-to-face meetings, where they can provide clients with compelling solutions that meet their needs and then skillfully move them through the sales process.

In the legal profession, litigators practice their craft by conducting moot court proceedings. In sales, we perfect *our* skills by re-enacting sales scenarios during structured training exercises. Sue used "mock" sales meetings to sharpen her team's presentation skills. She says, "We'd gather together in a conference room, where I'd ask someone to stand up and present one of our company's solutions. The rest of us would pretend we were members of a typical client's decision team, asking questions and raising objections relevant to the roles we were playing. The 'finance' representative among us would question the costs. The IT representative would probe for technical flaws. The presenter's goal was to deal with these challenges effectively while moving the 'client' to the next stage of the sales cycle. Afterward, we'd switch roles and have someone else be the presenter. It was a tremendous learning experience for everyone."

This kind of real-world practice is invaluable. It enables you to become increasingly adept at fielding difficult questions and anticipating issues that might otherwise blindside you in real life. You gain an ease and familiarity in describing the benefits of your solutions clearly and concisely. This pays huge dividends later when you actually meet with clients.

Keeping Your Vision Alive

It's natural to feel discouraged when you encounter a serious set-back. Sue remembers how hard it was for her to recover her vision and focus after her first bid to summit Everest.

> When I returned to Seattle, I felt like a failure. I keenly felt the loss of the goal that had filled me with energy and purpose throughout the previous year. For months afterward, I mulled over my Everest experience, questioning my desire to return for a second try. After all, Everest is extremely dangerous, with 250 climbers having lost their lives on its treacherous slopes. It requires a huge commitment of time, effort, and the opportunity costs of being away from home, family, friends, and work.
>
> One day, after a business meeting in Colorado Springs, I stopped by the Olympic Training Center for a quick tour. There I read the words: "If you can see it, you can perform it." Surrounded by photos of exceptional athletes and their struggles to win med-als, I was deeply moved and freshly motivated. My vision returned stronger than ever.
>
> Back home, I wrote down a new goal for my return to Everest. I would complete a hundred outdoor hikes within the next twelve months. But how, I wondered, would I achieve this while leading my sales team? I began by breaking this goal down into a series of manageable steps.
>
> Every week I would complete two demanding hikes. This goal was realistic. Twelve months later, I had met my goal and climbed over 300,000 vertical feet in the process. I was ready to return to Everest. Perfect plan, perfect preparation!

Commit to Your Vision

It's never too early to commit to your vision. If you want to run a race, sign up and pay the entry fee. If you want to become a top sales performer, tell yourself and your leader, *"I will nail my objective and stand on top."* Without commitment, your dream will never become a reality.

Sue and John's good friend Jim Whittaker demonstrates the kind of commitment that leads to high achievement. Prior to 1963, no American had successfully climbed Mount Everest. At the time, Jim was the general manager of REI, a small but fast-growing Seattle co-op that sold climbing gear and returned profits to members. So Jim was thrilled when he was invited to join the 1963 Everest expedition by Norman Dyhrenfurth, the leader.

"I'd never been to the Himalayas," says Whittaker. "But I'd reached the 20,320-foot summit of McKinley. I'd trained hard, wearing a sixty-pound backpack. I swam in Lake Sammamish in winter to acclimate myself to extreme cold. I didn't know anyone who was in better shape."

A number of other prospective climbers were interviewed the summer before the trip and asked if they expected to reach the summit. Most of them replied "I hope so," or "I'm going to do my best." Whittaker's response was both direct and unambiguous. "Yeah, I will."

Jim saw himself standing on the summit of Everest. He had committed to his vision. As a result, he would go on to become the first American to climb Everest.

If you follow Jim's example, you too can reach the peak of your profession. Top performers commit to success, sometimes years before they finally achieve it. The keys are vision, a realistic plan, and the perseverance to follow it through.

Focus Your Team on the Summit Vision

The best sales leaders are more than top performers. They've learned to think like a CEO. They inspire and lead by example. They demonstrate that it's possible to overcome your perceived limitations when you commit, without reservation, to your vision of success.

On the mountain, we say you must "lead from the front of the rope." To accomplish this in sales, we must be in the field walking the talk.

Sue's early experiences as a major account representative served her well when she became a sales leader and management increased her team's revenue objective from $250 million to $300 million. Somehow she and her team would have to increase their productivity, despite having fewer people than the year before.

My team experienced severe sticker shock when I informed them about their new objective. "This is ridiculous," they complained. "We can't work any harder than we did last year. This is impossible!"

I explained that the market opportunity for the industry exceeded a trillion dollars. "That makes $300 million both realistic and achievable. We just have to increase our slice of the pie."

I urged them to focus on this vision during the coming year. "Put the number aside for now. It's just a number," I told them. "We're going to focus on what we always focus on. We're going to be the top performing team. At the end of the year, all of you will be recognized for your great work. Picture yourself being congratulated by executive management."

Afterward I sat down with each member of my team to prepare a detailed plan for the yearlong campaign ahead. I held mandatory team reviews and informal huddles every week to track their progress against goals and keep their vision alive through repetition.

It's critically important to keep your goals front and center on an ongoing basis. So I created a visual for my team that depicted a mountain with our $300 million objective standing at the summit.

I also created a fifty-two-week series of "climbing goals" that would enable the team to reach the summit.

During the weekly sales meetings, I asked each team member where they stood in relation to their personal summit goal. Then I added up everyone's numbers and plugged them into that week's "revenue base camp."

If anyone was falling short, I'd ask for specific details about what they were going to do and what support they needed to get back on track. If someone was meeting their goal, I would ask them to help their teammates by describing their campaigns and explaining why they were succeeding. This enabled them to develop a set of best sales practices that benefitted everyone. It also gave me an opportunity to provide whatever help someone needed to blow away their numbers.

These kinds of sales meetings have a number of practical benefits. They keep everyone focused on a common goal. They build a sense of teamwork and mutual support. And they help everyone learn what works and what doesn't, so they can be as efficient and productive as possible.

If you hold a leadership position as a sales executive or entrepreneur, we suggest you adapt Sue's techniques to strengthen *your* team and help members achieve their goals. And, if you're a member of a team like this, consider asking your team leader to implement a similar program. In either case, you'll be surprised and delighted by the rapid and ongoing improvements you'll see in your team's performance.

The best leaders lead by example. So Sue made it a point to work harder than ever before to develop her own new account opportunities and to support her team every step of the way in their campaigns. The results were extraordinary. Sue led her sales team to achieve 150 percent of its $300 million revenue objective. Against all odds, they had realized—and exceeded—their vision.

Measure the Mountain: Holding Yourself Accountable

You've acquired a vision and defined a set of realistic goals for achieving it. Next it's essential to monitor your progress, a process we refer to as Measuring the Mountain.

Metrics allow us to evaluate results and make necessary adjustments and course corrections. In climbing, we keep journals. In sales, we use dashboards and scorecards to keep us on track.

Jay Tyler, John's former district sales manager at Xerox Corporation, puts it this way: "You can only manage your attitude and activities." Activities constitute your daily "to do" list. Review this at the beginning and end of each day. Did you make as many prospecting calls as you planned? Did you check in with all of your prospects? Don't fool yourself. If you fall short one day, then you must double up the next.

> *Peak sales performers constantly measure everything: the number of face-to-face meetings with clients, the number of new contacts developed each week, quota achievement, and pipeline opportunities. . . .*
> —*Anthony Orlando, senior vice president of CA Technologies*

Think BIG!

While goals need to be attainable, they must also stretch you to the limit and inspire you to achieve something truly ambitious, something that you deeply care about. If not, you'll give up too easily when you encounter obstacles. Aim too low and you'll become a complacent midtier performer. Aim too high and you'll fall short and become discouraged and deflated. But if you realistically assess yourself and the scope of the opportunity before you, then our CLIMB methodology will lead you to heights of achievement you never thought possible.

John spent six productive years at Verizon (formerly GTE). During the first three years, he was instrumental in forming and then rapidly expanding the company's data communications sales division. In his first five years, he consistently attained his annual quota and was twice recognized as a member of the Winner's Circle, the firm's highest achievement, which was awarded to the top performing 3 percent of the company's highly skilled sales force.

Although he was determined to leave Verizon and earn an MBA, John resolved to remain one final year to achieve his most ambitious vision yet: to join the elite ranks of the top one percent in sales. For the next twelve months, he set aggressive goals and attacked them with a new level of intensity and commitment. He measured his progress and made corrections, redoubling his efforts whenever he felt his forward momentum starting to stall. He simply refused to give up.

When the year ended, he had attained his vision. He was the top salesperson in his region and among the top one percent in the country.

As she advanced in her career, Sue also continued to dream big. First, she would climb the corporate ladder to become director of sales, where she helped her team exceed its $300 million revenue objective. Then she would lead the top performing sales team as vice president of sales at a technology industry leader. And finally, she would climb Mount Everest and fulfill her Seven Summits dream.

In this chapter, we discussed the power of committing to a vision and then letting that vision drive your activity. We talked about setting realistic goals that reflect your self-assessment of your professional and personal development and sticking with these goals when the going gets tough. And we emphasized the importance of measuring your progress and the joy and fulfillment that comes with achieving your dreams.

In the chapters to come, we'll discuss the concrete skills and attitudes you must develop to become a top sales performer, utilizing the Project. Prepare. Persevere principles we've developed as sales executives and mountain climbers. For now, remember that top performers:

✓ Project their future.

✓ Write down their summit goals.

✓ Commit to a vision that is Concise, Levelheaded, Integrated, Measurable, and Big.

✓ Keep their vision alive through repetition.

✓ Become an expert in a key area or industry segment.

✓ Never let discomfort divert them from achieving goals that are realistic!

✓ Always let their vision drive their activity.

✓ Hold themselves accountable by measuring the mountain.

2

TRAVEL LIGHT

During climbing season, Base Camp on the southern slope of Mount Everest is festooned with tents draped in colorful prayer flags. Here, at approximately 17,600 feet, mountaineers from across the globe prepare for the summit by making a series of slow climbs to and from Camps II and III. These repeated journeys, to altitudes reaching 24,000 feet, are essential because they enable climbers to acclimate their bodies to low oxygen conditions, to prepare the mountain with fixed ropes, and to establish Camp IV (or High Camp, at 26,000 feet), where they will ultimately make their final push for the summit.

At 19,000 feet, Camp I is the first stop above the Khumbu Icefall, a frozen river that flows approximately four feet per day. This stretch is among the most challenging and dangerous sections of the five discrete climbs that collectively make up the South Col route to the summit. At the Icefall, climbers encounter towering blocks of ice the size of small buildings that are split by deep crevasses diving hundreds of feet to the earth below. These icy behemoths—known as "seracs"—are constantly on the move, crashing and splitting apart on their paths downstream.

Traversing beneath seracs is extremely dangerous, since the route is constantly changing. Here, as on the rest of Everest, climbers rely on the Sherpa, an ethnic group from Nepal who have a genetic adaptation that gives them a unique ability to accommodate high altitudes while serving as porters and guides. Among climbers, the Sherpa are as renowned for their strength and climbing skill as for their warmth and selflessness, making them essential members of virtually every Everest summit team.

Climbing the Khumbu Icefall. *(Sue Ershler)*

Sherpa teams work diligently to piece together a safe route, spanning the crevasses with a bridge of sixty or more ordinary aluminum garden ladders strung one after another. Climbing teams will typically make a minimum of four round-trips through the Icefall during an expedition, never seeing the same route twice.

The ladders sway, bounce, and seem to laugh ominously, emitting creaks and groans as they shift in the slow-moving current. Climbers try to navigate this treacherous section as quickly as possible. But at this altitude, every step you take feels like running a marathon with a pillow tied around your face. Every extra pound you carry can spell the difference between survival and meeting a frozen death within the Khumbu Glacier. Sue recalls her first foray into the Icefall:

I prepared extra carefully, packing and repacking my gear. The climbing was slow and tedious as I navigated the fall's frozen intricacies. It was rough going. My pack felt as if it had been filled with lead. I was sluggish and nervous. Finally, mentally and physically exhausted, I made it safely to Camp I.

I knew that something would have to change if I hoped to repeat this round-trip journey several more times without incident. When I shared my concerns with a fellow climber over a cup of tea, he responded by rooting around in my pack, pulling out my toothbrush, and snapping it in half! At sea level, I would have been astonished and more than a bit annoyed. Here, I was thankful.

The weight savings was minimal but the lesson was profound. I realized that I had been treating Everest as if it were different from every other mountain I had climbed. Because I feared it, I had overcompensated by packing more gear than I really needed. I realized that Everest was just another mountain, one that required the same "one step at a time" approach that had brought me success in the past.

After that, I crossed the Icefall several times carrying only the precise amount of food, clothing, and even aspirin tablets I would need that day. I grew in confidence and strength. I had learned to Travel Light—to take what you need to get the job done and nothing more.

As we discussed in chapter 1, every success begins with a clearly defined vision supported by a concise set of achievable goals. We emphasized that successful salespeople set goals that are realistic and measurable. Then they commit without compromise to achieving them.

How can *you* achieve *your* goals? In this chapter, we'll begin to answer that question. We'll start with concrete strategies to help you transform your overarching vision into a workable action plan. We'll consider the obstacles you may encounter in setting and adhering to your priorities and how you can most effectively overcome these potential pitfalls to success. We'll point out the difference between daily activities that are strategic and those that are merely tactical.

(Mike Ellerman)

We'll delineate an approach to sales that allows you to focus your precious time, energy, and resources where they'll do you the most good. In short, we'll explain the importance of Traveling Light: The Second Summit of Sales Success.

Start with Your Vision and Work Backward

Once our vision to climb Everest was firmly established, we began to consider how to accomplish it. We resolved to **work backward**, an approach to achievement that can be as effective in your professional life as it is on the mountain. In this case, we broke our vision down into seven "subgoals," beginning with our final one: to reach the summit by mid-May. Then we worked backward, step by step, defining each of the six additional subgoals we would need to complete along the way. This approach is illustrated in *Figure 1*.

Figure 1: Working Backward to Climb Everest

Goal	Deadline	Description	Time frame
7. Reach summit: 29,035 ft.	Mid-May	All camps are in position, our bodies are ready, and the mountain is fixed with ropes for safety.	2–3 days from Camp IV
6. Establish five camps	Late March–late April	Base Camp established mid-March, followed by Camps I–IV.	March 15–May 1
5. Fix the mountain with safety ropes	May 1	Ropes connect all camps to the route to the summit.	April 1–May 1

Goal	Deadline	Description	Time frame
4. Acclimatize our bodies	May 1	Complete several climbs between Base Camp and Camp I to accelerate the production of red blood cells needed to "go high."	March 15–May 1
3. Final preparations for departure	March 18	Assemble and pack the technical gear and supplies needed for the climb.	March 1–15
2. Physical conditioning	March 18	Complete rigorous training regimen with frequent climbs to prepare physically for Everest.	October–March
1. Visualize ourselves standing on top of the world	July	Make a daily habit of visualizing ourselves standing atop Everest.	From the moment we decided to reach the summit.
Total time to climb Mount Everest	8 months, 14 days		

De-Clutter Your Life and Set Priorities

In climbing, there's no ambiguity about the need to travel light. The more weight you carry, the harder your journey will be. In sales, this takes on another meaning.

We're living in an age of information overload. As salespeople, we're burdened with blizzards of e-mails, endless meetings, and countless demands on our time. It can be all too easy to become overwhelmed. Suddenly we may look up and discover that our best-laid plans to focus on revenue-generating activities have been derailed. But it doesn't have to be this way. The key to success is to de-clutter both our personal and professional lives. In short, we have to take some of the weight out of our backpacks!

How can *you* do this? The first step is to jettison everything that stands in the way of your ultimate vision of blowing away your quota and becoming a top performer. That means setting priorities every day and then completing every task needed to fulfill them as efficiently as possible.

Start every morning by carefully assessing which activities must be accomplished that day, which can wait, which can be delegated, and, best of all, which can be eliminated entirely.

"I do that already," you may be grumbling to yourself as you read this. Every day, you diligently compile a "to do" list of everything that's on your plate. But, if you're like many salespeople, your list is an unstructured collection of tasks that don't reflect the priorities required to achieve your vision or provide a realistic time frame for completing them. Lists like these simply don't work.

As salespeople, we should think of our "to do" items as physical objects that we place in our backpacks to help us achieve our daily mission. We must pack with care and purpose. Just as Sue learned to carry only the precise number of aspirin tablets she needed, we must learn to delay, eliminate, or reassign any activity that doesn't help us ascend "Mount Quota."

High-priority tasks are usually the most difficult ones, so they create the heaviest loads. These are the phone calls we don't want to make, the industry research we need to conduct to understand a new client's business requirements, or the meeting with a prospect who now seems to be leaning toward a competitor.

If you're like most salespeople, you may find yourself focusing primarily on easy tasks. You probably devote too much time to doing busywork, attending unproductive meetings, and in general, reacting to other people's priorities. Just think how many sales you could have closed if you had spent that time meeting with prospective clients instead.

Don't fool yourself. Afternoon fatigue is not necessarily caused by a lack of caffeine. It's caused by the debilitating load that's been on your back since you first scribbled down your "to do" list that morning. You've been hauling around an anchor all day. Your heaviest, most difficult tasks are still right there, lying at the bottom of your pack.

Planning Your Day: Thirty Minutes at Base Camp

There's a better way. Every morning you should plan on holding a thirty-minute packing session. Let's call it "thirty minutes at Base Camp." During this session you'll create a list of every activity you could conceivably focus on that day. Include everything, especially the difficult tasks that are keeping you up at night.

Envision where you need to be at the end of the day in order to consider it a success. What tasks must you accomplish to meet that goal? Make sure they're all listed. These are your high-priority items. Remember we're working backward.

Next, transfer only the highest-priority items to your daily calendar. Carefully evaluate how long it will take to complete each one. If they don't fit within your time constraints, reprioritize until you get it right. Don't overpack. Be realistic.

Although only high-priority items will make it to your calendar that day, don't worry. You'll return to your comprehensive "to do" list during subsequent Base Camp sessions, repacking every day, adding new activities, and removing others. Your load will steadily lighten as you prioritize, eliminate, delegate, and accomplish.

On the mountain, it seems as if we're continually packing, unpacking, and repacking in our ongoing attempts to find the optimal load. During *your* "thirty minutes at Base Camp" session, try to pack and repack only once. Don't overthink it. Now, start climbing!

Figures 2 and 3 illustrate the Base Camp planning process.

Comprehensive "To Do" List Activities	Priority	Delegate	Eliminate	Time Required
Research new industry for upcoming sales call	High			2 hours
Client meeting—discuss proposal	High			1.5 hours
Complete expense report—due today	High	X		30 minutes
Send flowers to sister for her birthday	High	X		15 minutes
Work out, get a bite	High			1.5 hours
Base Camp planning session	High			30 minutes
Prospecting calls	High			1 hour
Contact existing clients to assess satisfaction/needs	High			1 hour
Read and respond to internal e-mails	Medium			1 hour
Return personal calls, e-mails, texts	Medium			1 hour
Buy wine for party in two weeks	Low	X		1 hour
Upload business trip photos to Facebook	Low		X	30 minutes
Online shopping	Low		X	30 minutes

Figure 2: Your Starting "Prepack" "To Do" List

	Repacked Activities	Calendar and Climb!
1	Read industry white paper over morning coffee	6:00 a.m.–6:30 a.m.
2	Arrive at the office	7:15 a.m.
3	Send flowers to sister for her birthday	7:15 a.m.–7:30 a.m.
4	Thirty-minute Base Camp planning	7:30 a.m.–8:00 a.m.
5	Client meeting—discuss proposal	8:00 a.m.–9:30 a.m.
6	Prospecting calls	10:00 a.m.–11:00 a.m.
7	Contact existing clients to assess satis-faction/needs	11:00 a.m.–12:00 p.m.
8	Work out, get a bite, personal calls, and e-mails	12:00 p.m.–1:30 p.m.
9	Revise proposal (due 5:00 p.m.) and draft follow-up e-mails to client, support team, and sales leadership	1:30 p.m.–3:30 p.m.
10	Research new industry for upcoming sales call	3:30 p.m.–5:30 p.m.
11	Complete expense report—due today	5:30 p.m.–6:00 p.m.
12	Read and respond to internal e-mails	6:00 p.m.–7:00 p.m.
13	Shop for groceries and home for dinner	7:00 p.m.–8:30 p.m.
14	Update master "to do" list to prepare for tomorrow's Base Camp planning session	8:30 p.m.–9:00 p.m.
15	Upload new pictures to Facebook	9:00 p.m.–9:30 p.m.

Figure 3: Your Prioritized "Repacked" "To Do" List

Not All Activities Are Created Equal

We've discussed how setting priorities enables you to achieve your daily goals. We've learned how to structure each day to focus on "vision-driven" activities. If we follow this regimen faithfully—stringing together days of steady accomplishment the way the Sherpas bridge the Khumbu Icefall—we're sure to reach new heights of sales success.

Now it's time to dig a little deeper. We know that some vision-driven activities are more important than others. However, we must also learn to distinguish between those that are strategic and those that are merely tactical.

Tactical Activities

While you're conducting your daily thirty-minute Base Camp sessions, look for tasks that can be handled quickly or delegated, perhaps to a virtual assistant. Use your Sherpas! The art of delegating and outsourcing is essential to Traveling Light.

Although they're often tedious and administrative, tactical tasks should never be put off or completed piecemeal. Your objective should be to hit it and complete it. Consider e-mail, for example. Read each message just once. Be efficient. Your choices are limited: delete, reply, forward, or file. Follow the same drill for paper files—and recycle!

Take the same approach with tactical customer-oriented tasks. Some you can delegate. Others must be performed with a sense of urgency. Remember, even the most mundane, seemingly insignificant customer interaction reflects on you and your company.

Examples of Tactical Activities

- Administrative
  - Completing expense reports
  - Maintaining an orderly office and desk space
  - Submitting health care claims and forms
  - Attending mandatory internal meetings

- Customer-Oriented
  - Following up on a service call
  - Introducing clients to company executives
  - Attending industry and social events with customers
  - Returning client e-mails and phone calls

- Personal
  - Picking up your dry cleaning
  - Shopping for groceries
  - Monitoring social media sites

Strategic Activities

Distinguishing between activities that are tactical and those that are strategic can be difficult for some sales professionals, especially when they're new to the field. John remembers a defining moment early in his career that would prove critical to his future success.

> I began my sales career at Xerox Corporation. After completing several months of training, I was thrilled to be assigned my first territory. I proceeded to make hundreds of cold calls before finding my first real prospect.
>
> Rushing back to the office, I began drafting the elaborate proposal I was convinced would seal the deal. I knew that spending

time in the office during business hours was generally frowned upon. So I wasn't surprised when a sales manager approached me and asked why I was at my desk instead of out in the field.

Expecting praise, I described the wonderful opportunity I'd found and explained that my proposal was the critical final step in making my first copier sale. The sales manager listened politely and then shocked me by saying, "You've already lost. If this prospect is really that ready to buy, one of our competitors is with them right now closing the deal."

The sales manager was right. What I *should* have done was ask for the order, field objections, and then get the deal signed there and then. It was a bitter lesson, but an important one.

Strategic activities are the key to achieving long-term, top performer status. Properly understood and approached, they will help you reach the summit of sales achievement and remain there throughout your career.

Strategic activities provide you with a competitive edge and help you build customer loyalty. They encompass such activities as continuously enhancing your industry knowledge, educating yourself about your products and services, and understanding how they stack up against the competition. Strategic activities are designed to help you craft compelling value propositions and pursue the holy grail of consultative-based selling. Clients will appreciate your commitment to helping them achieve their own professional success. You will build long-term relationships that sustain you throughout your career.

Examples of Strategic Activities

- Professional Development
  - Reading industry white papers
  - Attending industry conferences
  - Seeking—and meeting with—industry experts and mentors

- Customer-Oriented
  - Sharing your industry knowledge during customer meetings
  - Attending customer events and strategic summits
  - Providing customers with introductions to industry contacts

- Personal
  - Creating and adhering to a fitness and wellness plan
  - Maintaining strong family and personal relationships

Achieving a Balance

No one can or should work all the time. Peak performers strive to maintain a healthy balance between their personal and professional lives. So they apply the same Travel Light principles we've been discussing to integrate the two. When you repack your daily calendar, it should also include activities like doctor's visits, lunches with friends, and, of course, personal fitness. A vigorous hike or bike ride outside in the fresh air will bring new perspectives to *all* of the tasks weighing down your backpack.

As keynote speakers, we've had the pleasure of meeting top sales performers from almost every industry sector. We're always struck by how similar they are in their approach to achieving life balance. Sue was reminded of this recently when she presented to a group of top one percent award-winning financial consultants who had achieved elite status as their company's best and most productive salespeople.

When asked how they balanced their professional and personal lives, each of these top performers described a formal process or system they had adopted for managing their time and staying focused on the right activities. Many had taken time-management courses. All of them used the strategies and techniques we've described in this chapter. You can do the same to achieve top performer status in *your* career.

Sue recently went on a hike with Robyn Garrison, one of the highest-ranking female executives at Boeing. Although she has an extraordinarily busy work schedule, Robyn still found time to climb several of the Seven Summits. Her secret: Robyn starts her day at 4:30 a.m. She sets climbing goals to drive her workouts, sets her daily calendar to reflect work and family priorities, and then compartmentalizes. Family. Work. Fitness. These are her top priorities. When she is pursuing one of them, she goes 100 percent. The other facets of her life simply have to wait!

Be true to balance. When you're working, give it everything you've got. When you're playing, go for it 100 percent. The same holds true for every other aspect of your life. Constructive activities feed off one another, making you more productive in every facet of your life. During his Seven Summits journey, John also ran eleven marathons while continuing to excel in his business career.

As we've seen, you need an overarching vision, clearly defined goals, and a disciplined system of vision-driven activities to succeed in sales. This has always been true, but never more so than today, when sales professionals are besieged by information overload and mounting demands on their time. It's noisier than ever out there.

Technology has afforded us new and exciting productivity tools. On the one hand, smartphones, tablet computers, and other technology tools can be real time-savers, allowing us to become more efficient and productive in everything we do. But unless we apply the principles of Traveling Light, they can also introduce new clutter and distractions into our lives. Tools are just a means to an end. We need to wield them properly if we wish to excel.

Technological advancements have now found their way to Mount Everest too. Only a decade ago, satellite telephone service at Base Camp was iffy at best. Today, climbers watch movies on flat-screen TVs and sip from mugs of steaming espresso while instant messaging friends and colleagues around the world.

Still, technology hasn't changed the basic reality on the ground. The mountain is still 29,035 feet high. Climbing is still challenging, rigorous, and at times treacherous. To reach the summit, we must distinguish between activities that help us achieve our goals and those that don't. Whether we're preparing to reach the summit or exceed our sales quotas, there's only so much room in our pack. We all need to Travel Light!

In this chapter, we showed you how Traveling Light enables you to focus on your most important daily activities while also maintaining a balance in your life. In subsequent chapters, we'll delve into strategic and tactical activities in greater detail. For now, remember to:

✓ Never lose sight of your **vision and goals**.

✓ **Work backward** to determine what you need to accomplish every day.

✓ Start every morning with a **thirty minutes at Base Camp** exercise that allows you to pack only what you need that day.

✓ **Prioritize** activities that truly drive your vision—create your own system of vision-driven activities.

✓ Accept that you can't necessarily get everything done in one day, but that you can always get the **right things** done!

✓ Fill your backpack with **client-facing** activities.

✓ **Eliminate** and **delegate** noncritical activities, especially administrative tasks.

✓ **De-clutter!** Be efficient and decisive with your files and correspondence.

✓ Take advantage of **productivity tools** such as a virtual assistant.

✓ **Compartmentalize** to maintain focus.

✓ Don't forget to **work out**! This will provide clarity and perspective!

PART II

PREPARE

3

PLAN THE ROUTE

Mount McKinley–Denali *(Phil Ershler)*

PREPARE: No big mountain is scaled in a single climb. No quota is achieved in a single day. You must create a strategic plan that delineates every step of your journey and includes metrics to measure success along the way. Your sales quota is *your* big mountain.

In preparing for battle, I have always found that plans are useless, but planning is indispensable.

—*General Dwight D. Eisenhower*

At 20,320 feet, Alaska's Mount McKinley is the tallest mountain in North America and one of the most challenging of the Seven Summits. The historical name, Denali, which translates to "The High One" or "The Great One," aptly describes McKinley's massive size and the vastness of its frozen wilderness. Temperatures routinely dip as low as −80°F, with wind chills reaching −120° F.

Flowing off Denali's two major summits on the north and south are five immense glaciers. The Kahiltna Glacier, which provides a route up the southwest side of Denali, is the starting point for most climbers attempting to summit North America's highest peak. It is on the Kahiltna Glacier that small airplanes, equipped with skis to land on ice and snow, drop climbers off to begin their journey. If they are successful, the climbers will reunite with the pilots on the glacier after approximately three weeks of navigating Denali's frozen wilderness to the mountain's summit.

To climb Denali, most climbers train on Washington State's Mount Rainier, the most glaciated mountain in the lower forty-eight states. John and Sue had summited Rainier many times, but Denali—at almost 6,000 feet higher than Rainier—coupled difficult technical conditions with dangerous altitude. It has been said that Rainier is a junior Denali and that Denali is a junior Everest. Everest was in their future, but Alaska's Denali was a prerequisite to achieving their goal of climbing the world's highest peaks.

On July 3, 1995, Sue, her husband and expedition guide Phil, John, and their friend Andy Lufkin landed on the Kahiltna Glacier, unloaded their massive loads of gear, food, and supplies, and took their first look at the imposing mountain they had set out to climb. Denali and the surrounding mountains, glaciers, granite rock walls, and valleys combined to form a forbidding and ominous environment.

Each of the climbers carried a heavy backpack and wore a harness that was attached to a sled packed with additional gear.

Slowly, the team began to make their way to Camp 1, where they would eat, drink, and sleep in preparation for the first stage of the climb. Almost immediately, however, they realized they were in trouble. At five foot two, Sue was simply unable to carry so much weight while keeping pace with the other climbers as they crossed several deadly crevasse fields. She struggled to keep up, fighting back tears as she gasped for breath in the thin air. On more than one occasion, Sue had outclimbed men on Mount Rainier, but now she questioned her ability to complete this climb and confronted the very real possibility that she might fail, or even die, on Denali.

Fortunately, as good leaders always do, Phil sensed her struggle and offered her the support she needed. "Don't worry," he told her. "We're not going to climb the whole mountain in one day. Just take it one step at a time. We'll follow our plan and climb in stages." The team encouraged Sue, transferred some of her supplies to their sleds, and resumed their trek. For the next few hours, Sue focused all of her energy on reaching Camp 1. When that failed to sustain her motivation, she concentrated on making it to the next break. When that no longer worked, she narrowed her focus to simply taking one step after the next. Finally, after what felt like an eternity, the team made it safely to Camp 1.

Afterward, Phil addressed the team. "Today was hard," he told them. "But if we follow our plan to climb in stages, from camp to camp, one step at a time, we'll be successful." He reminded them that expedition climbing is like eating an elephant one bite at a time. On that first day, the team had taken their first bite and survived. In the days to come, Sue would regain her energy and confidence and achieve her goal of standing triumphantly with her team at Denali's summit. Remember, our vision creates the goal, but we need to establish a well-thought-out plan and execute each step within the plan to realize our goals.

Planning for Success in Sales

In chapters 1 and 2, we discussed the essential role that *projecting* your vision and goals plays in helping you prioritize the daily activities that can lead to high achievement in sales. In this chapter, we will *prepare* you to become a top performer by providing you with a set of systematic planning processes. We'll begin by reviewing the concept of "solution selling," how it has evolved over the past decade, and how planning fits into the modern solution selling paradigm.

Decades ago, selling was almost exclusively product-oriented. The salesperson had a widget to sell and a prospect to sell it to. The goal was simple: persuade the prospect to buy the widget, based on its superior attributes. No consideration was given to whether the prospect actually needed the item. Not surprisingly, this approach proved to be both inefficient and unproductive.

Solution selling reversed the process by shifting the focus from the product to the customer. Now the salesperson's first goal was to assess the prospect's needs and identify the business problem to be solved. Only then would the salesperson attempt to provide a customized set of products and services. Solution selling allowed us to get to know our customers and their needs and to sell *solutions*, not simply *products*.

The Xerox Corporation mastered the art of solution selling in the 1980s by employing the strategic sales techniques first introduced by Neil Rackham in his groundbreaking book, *SPIN® Selling*, which was based on the massive twelve-year research study he spearheaded with the help of thirty researchers in more than twenty countries. SPIN, which would be cloned and modified over the next three decades, is an acronym for **Situation, Problem, Implication, and Need**. It encompasses a comprehensive selling model, training regimen, and planning process.

In the **Situation** phase, salespeople focus on developing an in-depth understanding of the decision maker and their business by asking probing questions about their organizational processes, products, work flow, competitors, profit opportunities, employees, work groups, systems (human and technical), successes, and challenges. The goal is to identify and prioritize the most pressing **Problems** the salesperson can solve with his or her firm's products and services. This approach, which focuses primarily on soliciting information from the prospect, is referred to as Extraction.

Implications describes the concrete, quantifiable effects of the business problems identified during the Situation and Problem phases. These might include lost revenues or profits, reduced productivity, a demoralized workforce, and the loss of market share or competitive capability. Only after this process is complete is the salesperson ready to tailor and present a value proposition that addresses the prospect's fully defined and quantified **Needs**.

Moving from Extraction to Education

Solution selling has evolved a good deal since the SPIN model was first introduced. Over the past decade, clients have become much more sophisticated and demanding. They now require solutions that position them to exploit emerging market trends and opportunities. Today, the most successful salespeople do more than simply extract—they *educate and guide* their clients.

As Thomas Edison once said, "Good fortune is what happens when opportunity meets with planning." This is especially true when it comes to sales.

But how do you create a plan that brings about business transformation? What does such a plan look like? How can you track your activities and change course when you encounter obstacles? The three key components of an optimal plan are:

1. *Reflect and Reload.* In this component, we assess our previous performance and set new goals for meeting our upcoming sales

objectives. We also reflect on what we've learned in the field, from our research, and from our customers.

2. **The Inside Route.** In this component, we assess our readiness to craft solutions by setting goals for expanding our knowledge of our company, products, and services.

3. **The Outside Route.** In this component, we employ the **Who, What**, and **Where** considerations that define the selling environment and our selling targets.

Planning Component 1: Reflect and Reload

Before we can set new performance goals, we must first establish a baseline by making a frank assessment of our previous performance based on an objective set of performance metrics. We can then address any deficiencies by creating a new set of performance goals that should be achieved during the coming year. We refer to this as Reflecting and Reloading.

See the chart below for a simple example of a self-assessment by a fictional salesperson, Jason Smith.

Plan	Annual Quota (objective)	Annual Performance	% of Plan
Annual Sales Quota (revenue)	$500,000	$457,000	91.4%
New Customer Meetings	96 meetings	80 meetings	83.3%
Customer Presentations	50 presentations	37 presentations	74.0%

Plan	Annual Quota (objective)	Annual Performance	% of Plan
System "A" Product Sales	30	27	90.0%
System "B" Product Sales	10	2	20.0%

In column one, Jason has listed the performance metrics he resolved to track one year ago. As we can see, Jason met 91.4 percent of his quota. Not bad, but hardly top performer status. Jason didn't make President's Club last year, but he's not about to lose his job, either.

The numbers, however, are quite revealing. Jason fell far short of his goal for new customer meetings and performed even worse with respect to customer presentations. An increase in activities in these areas should lead to increased sales and revenue. Another glaring issue is Jason's failure to sell his firm's System B product. Virtually all of his sales were for System A. Why has he underperformed so badly?

Jason has been selling System A for years. He knows it backward and forward. But System B is based on new technology he doesn't fully understand. Jason finds it difficult to clearly explain System B's features and benefits. Worse, he's unable to extract information that might show when System B is a better fit for a client than System A. This chart makes it clear that Jason is selling products, not solutions. It's a wake-up call that should spur him to fully educate himself about System B. We'll consider these kinds of course corrections when we discuss the Inside Route.

But first, Jason should take the time to Reload by creating a new chart with his quota, goals, and objectives for the coming year. His revised worksheet should include a goal to master the technology and functionality information for System B so he can meet his sales quota.

Take a moment now to Reflect and create a similar chart for yourself. Review the professional goals you established for yourself in chapter 1 and incorporate them into your own Reload worksheet.

Now perform a qualitative assessment of your past sales period. You can use the same approach to review your personal goals. Did you attain the personal goals you set for yourself, such as running a half marathon or climbing your first mountain? Did you create a healthy balance between your work and personal life?

Achieving this balance will put you in a better position to succeed in your territory. Consider the following possibilities for enhancing your personal life and then complete the Reloading process with your own version.

✓ Complete a bike tour or running race.

✓ Reach out to an old friend once a month.

✓ Assess your diet and set a weight or fitness goal.

✓ Read one nonbusiness book every month.

✓ Learn to cook or to cook several new dishes.

✓ Take on a new hobby.

✓ Keep a journal.

✓ Travel somewhere new.

✓ Exercise every day.

Be sure to include specific performance metrics you can track and review when you start the Reflect/Reload cycle again next year.

Before embarking on the Denali expedition, John reflected on the problems he had encountered two years earlier when the team climbed Mount Elbrus, 18,510 feet, and the highest mountain on the European continent, located in the Caucasus mountain range near Russia.

At 18,510 feet, Elbrus challenges climbers with high altitudes, harsh conditions, and technical challenges similar to those found on Denali. The Elbrus climb had been my first ascent above 14,410 feet. It was also the first real test of my ability to acclimatize to the thin air and "go high." On the final day, our team was forced to climb nearly 5,000 feet from High Camp to the summit in the face of freezing temperatures, high winds, and unstable weather conditions. After a nightlong climb, we reached the summit. But it took all of my energy and will to keep up with them. After reaching the peak, I was too exhausted to safely descend at the pace set by the others. Soon, I was lagging behind my team, struggling with every step down the icy terrain. Noticing my distress, several of them waited for me, offering food, water, and encouragement. Finally, spent and demoralized, I made it back to High Camp.

Reflecting on my Elbrus experience, I concluded that my planning had been insufficient because I had not adequately defined my goal. My objective was not only to reach the summit, it was also to return safely to the bottom. I resolved to correct this mistake on Denali. So I Reloaded and embarked on an aggressive training regimen. When I landed on the Kahiltna Glacier, I was in far better physical condition than I had been on Elbrus. During the daily climbs, I avoided wasting precious energy on nonessentials. On summit day, I made sure to eat and drink at regular intervals, to climb only within my capacity, and to focus on the round trip. Thanks to my Reflect and Reload planning, the expedition was a great success.

Planning Component 2: The Inside Route

Now that you've completed your self-assessment and set goals for self-improvement, it's time to create an action plan to achieve them. It's time to plan the Inside Route. This will comprise an assessment of your company, products, and services, as well as a review of your prior successes and failures.

Know Your Company

There was a time when a gifted salesperson could rely on his or her charm and perseverance to close a deal. Those days are decidedly over. Today's decision makers are contending with limited resources and mounting information overload. They must quickly assess whether you're capable of servicing their needs. You may only get one shot at making the first cut. So it's essential to present your company and its capabilities with clarity and assurance. This requires careful planning and preparation.

The chart below will help you get started. Research each item. Practice until you can articulate the key points clearly and with poise.

Your Company	• Origin and history
	▪ Mission statement
	▪ Departments and their responsibilities
	▪ Organizational chart

Your Company
- Target markets
- Areas of expertise
- Competitive positioning
- Unique capabilities
- Value propositions
- Recent successes
- Customer references
- Recent media coverage
- Online resources and tools

This is not a onetime exercise. Many of these items will change as your company responds to market and competitive pressures. So it's essential to update your plan and refresh your understanding annually. Your knowledge and self-assurance will communicate your pride in your organization. Your enthusiasm about its successes will be infectious. You'll become interesting to your prospect. This is the first step to building a lasting client relationship.

Know Your Products

You're not just competing with other companies for a sale. You're also vying with your fellow salespeople for access to product specialists and other limited resources. You may find it difficult to secure these resources if you haven't adequately defined and qualified your opportunities. So knowing your products and services and being able to persuasively articulate their features and benefits is critical. This too takes preparation and planning.

Early in their careers, John and Sue worked for GTE (now Verizon), selling complex telecommunications and data communications systems to large corporations in the Pacific Northwest. Among their clients were such companies as Microsoft and Boeing.

Verizon had a huge product portfolio and vast resources. Account managers had access to engineers and staff with expertise in every product and system the company sold. It wasn't uncommon for a team of ten to enter a sales presentation and for each member to present in their specific area of expertise. At Verizon, account managers typically acted as coordinators, orchestrating and directing the sales cycle from initial contact through closing.

One day John and Sue's sales manager informed them that he considered this selling model to be flawed and obsolete. He felt that the selling process was becoming too fluid and unpredictable. An account manager couldn't always depend on having the right technical resource available when a question came up during a meeting. "Both of you are going to have to become product experts able to move the sales process along independently," he told them. Today, this is the reality for almost every salesperson.

How well do *you* know your company's products and services? If you're like our fictional salesperson, Jason, your expertise can undoubtedly be improved. Use the chart below to get started.

Products and Services Knowledge	• High-level product and service descriptions.
	• How they are different/fit together.
	• Technical functionality and specifications.
	• Examples of value propositions.
	• Competitive advantages.

Products and Services Knowledge	▪ Pricing information and options.
	▪ Required training and programs.
	▪ Implementation schedules and resources.
	▪ Customer installations and references.

If you spend quality time on the Inside Route, you'll be handsomely rewarded. You'll earn credibility with your clients, feel confident in meetings, and develop the knowledge you need to independently move the sales process toward a successful conclusion.

Planning Component 3: The Outside Route

Most salespeople never consider the two planning components we just discussed. Have you started creating your own Reflecting/Reloading and Inside Route plans? If so, give yourself a pat on the back. You're way ahead of the game and ideally positioned to move on to Component 3: The Outside Route.

This planning phase focuses on the outside world, where you meet with clients and close business. Like all good plans, your Outside Route plan should be simple, clear, and straightforward. We'll frame this planning process using the three Ws: **Who, What,** and **Where.**

- **Who** refers to your target industry, market, and territory, as well as the people you'll be calling on to close business. We'll show how to address this through a Market Plan.

- **What** refers to the nature and extent of your prospect's business challenges. It encompasses the SPIN (Situation, Problem,

Interest, and Need) considerations we discussed earlier. We'll show how to address them with your Account Plan.

- **Where** refers to the solutions you'll provide your clients: the destinations and business transformations you'll help them achieve, serving as a trusted advisor and industry expert. This can only be determined, on an opportunity-by-opportunity basis, at the conclusion of the solution selling process.

Building Your Market Plan

Most companies pursue sales across multiple industries and market segments. Whether you're an industry specialist or a jack-of-all-trades, you'll need to acquire domain and industry-specific expertise if you hope to be successful in sales. The best way to achieve this is to create a Market Plan for each of the segments in which you compete. Then you will need to act on this plan on an ongoing basis and to continually update it as circumstances change.

The chart below will help you get started. Research each item and then practice until you can articulate the key points clearly and concisely.

The Market Plan
- Industry overview, e.g., products and services, annual revenues, market segments, etc.
- Industry trends, history, standards, major participants, and your company's response to trends.
  - Trend example: health care services, including surging health care costs, aging populations overwhelming the system, care provided by nurses and physician's assistants, and shortages of primary-care physicians.

The Market Plan

- Key market challenges.

- Opportunities for your products and services.

- Important and relevant information, including a glossary of industry specific "buzzwords."

- Your specific target market(s). Within the wireless industry, for example, this might include cell phone service providers and smartphone manufacturers.

- Description of your target accounts within each of these markets. (For existing customers, you'll create and update Account Plans.) Focus on the top-tier clients in your industry. When you achieve success with them, the rest will follow.

- For each target account, list the names of the decision makers and key influencers, as well as the coaches who can help you understand and navigate the organization.

- Set quantifiable goals for calling on each account, maintaining existing relationships, and gaining market share. (Refer to "Planning Your Day: Thirty Minutes at Base Camp" in chapter 2 to review the process for prioritizing your daily activities.)

A well-designed Market Plan offers many benefits. It gives you the industry expertise you'll need for consultative selling and allows you to offer repeatable solutions that will delight your clients and streamline the selling process. The research you conduct to create your plan will also help you evaluate the size of your market opportunity and identify the largest and most profitable market segments and sales opportunities. You may discover that achieving a seemingly impossible quota is not only realistic, but also inevitable. Sue discovered this early in her career selling telecom and data communications systems.

> I realized that my two law firm clients had almost identical operational requirements. I began to research the legal market, learning how law firms work, how they communicate, and how well-designed systems can improve their efficiency and profitability. Before long, I was an expert on law firms and their system requirements. I began calling on the ten largest law firms in Seattle, sharing my industry knowledge and offering compelling value propositions for making new system purchases and upgrades. Over time, I closed business with 90 percent of the law firms in my target market.
>
> Delighted with this success, I turned my attention to another vertical market: K-12 education. I carefully studied how school districts function, how they utilize communications systems, and the operational and financial challenges they face as government-funded entities. Soon I was an expert on school district work flows and communications requirements. I proceeded to forge relationships with superintendents at all of the K-12 school districts in my Washington state territory, crafting consistent solutions that were a perfect fit for their needs and helping them formulate plans to secure funding. The results were exceptional. In three years, we increased our K-12 revenue from $1 million to $17 million. I earned the annual Regional Sales Manager of the Year award, and everyone on my team achieved President's Club distinction.

Today's top performing companies build solid market plans. Consider one of Sue's recent keynote clients, Persistent Systems, which builds next-generation technology products for industry heavyweights such as Microsoft, Oracle, and IBM. When asked how they managed to achieve dramatic growth and maintain it through significant downturns, company president Hari Haran answered, "One key element of our strategy is to focus on four vertical markets: banking, life sciences, telecom, and infrastructure service companies."

Building Your Account Plan

Whether you're a strategic salesperson with a few major accounts or have hundreds of clients in your territory, it's essential to develop a plan for every client and prospect that presents the most significant near-term revenue opportunities. Start by identifying your top ten to fifteen accounts. Then use the chart below to begin constructing an Account Plan for each of them.

The Account Plan

- An organizational chart and detailed company profile that includes divisions, subsidiaries, departments, decision makers, influencers and coaches, markets, and competitors. If the company is public, also include a summary of the financials, risk factors, and other useful information disclosed in its SEC filings.
- List and describe all of the company's systems, products, and services that are relevant to your sales campaign.
- Perform a SPIN analysis to identify each company's most pressing business problems.
- Create a solution designed to meet these needs and a preliminary schedule to implement it.
- Maintain meeting schedules and track outcomes.

As you can see, the Account Plan reflects the solution selling best practices we discussed earlier coupled with an action plan to bring each campaign to a successful conclusion. But a well-conceived Account Plan can do even more than this, as John proved during his tenure at Verizon. In his words:

> I had worked hard to forge a strong long-term relationship with the Metro division of the City of Seattle. Drawing on the in-depth knowledge I acquired building my Account Plan, I was able to close a series of extremely lucrative sales of telecommunications and data communications systems. This included a set of complex communications systems that connected the Transportation Group to its bus network.
>
> Unexpectedly, the City of Seattle was approached by a consultant, who convinced my executive contacts that the Metro division's communication systems should be replaced as soon as possible because they were antiquated and costly to maintain. The city hired the consultant to identify the new system requirements, create a request for proposal (RFP), select and short-list vendors, and manage the proposal analysis and award process. The RFP was subsequently developed and distributed to a number of qualified bidders, including Verizon.
>
> I felt strongly that the consultant was flat out wrong. The RFP was written as if all of Metro's systems were unusable and must be immediately replaced with new ones. In my view, wholesale change was overkill and would be extremely costly for the city to implement. The necessary system improvements could be made much more cost-effectively through selective upgrades. My Account Plan for the Metro group included a detailed road map for system maintenance and periodic upgrades. Rather than respond to the RFP, I arranged a meeting with my Metro and the City of Seattle contacts to present my plan.
>
> Thanks to my efforts in account maintenance and relationship

building, I had earned a high degree of credibility with the decision-making team. They agreed with my plan and threw out the RFP. The following year, Metro embarked on a full-system upgrade and awarded the entire project to Verizon without competitive bidding. The sale exceeded several million dollars over a multiyear period. I had won the deal because of my Account Plan.

Where Are We Taking Our Clients?

We've addressed the **Who** and **What** aspects of the three Ws that define the Outside Route. Now it's time to consider the final, and perhaps most important, one of all: **Where** are we taking our clients?

This requires more than simply learning enough about their industries, markets, and accounts to competently sell products, services, and solutions. Top performers also strive to help their clients anticipate the future and achieve business transformation. They solve problems their clients aren't even aware of yet. This topic is so important it merits its own chapter: chapter 4, "Guide Your Clients to Success."

> As John, Sue, Phil, and Andy walked the final yards to the plane that would begin their journey home from the Kahiltna Glacier, they came upon a climbing team that had been forced to turn back from the summit when one of the climbers started suffering from high-altitude cerebral edema (HACE), a severe and often fatal form of altitude sickness. One of their team explained that they had planned to climb Denali "Alpine Style," with a very quick ascent and descent, rather than "Expedition Style," with incremental ascents and descents between camps. Expedition Style helps climbers ward off HACE and other forms of altitude sickness by giving their bodies time to acclimatize to altitude changes. The unsuccessful team had lasted only one week before

they were forced to turn back. Phil and his team safely completed their round trip to Denali's summit in three weeks. Their plan worked: one step at a time.

Making Time to Plan

By now we hope you've come to appreciate the importance of planning and how much it contributes to success in sales. Of course, planning is essential at every level of an organization, from the mail room to the executive suite. Bill Gates, the cofounder of Microsoft, for example, spent one week alone every six months to Reflect, Reload, and plan for the future. As he told *Fortune* magazine in 2006, "Right now, I'm getting ready for Think Week. In May, I'll go off for a week and read a hundred or more papers from Microsoft employees that examine issues related to the company and the future of technology. I've been doing this for over twelve years." Few of us have the luxury of going off on a weeklong planning retreat. But you can certainly devote at least one full day to planning on an annual basis and then carve out time every week to review your progress and update your Market and Account plans. If you invest sufficient time and energy to planning your route, you're sure to reach the summit of sales success.

In this chapter, we moved beyond the Project phase, which focuses on setting goals, establishing priorities, and Traveling Light. In this first section of the Prepare phase, we laid down the essential foundations for creating successful plans. In our next chapter, "Guide Your Clients to Success," we'll delve into the skills top performers must develop and perfect in order to help their clients secure a long-term competitive advantage. For now, remember that:

✓ Simply selling a product's attributes fails to establish a **customer need**.

✓ Traditional "solution selling" only extracts problems and needs known to the customer, but it fails to **educate**.

✓ Top sales performers **plan** everything. They never wing it.

✓ Your plan must address the **three Ws**: **Who, What,** and **Where**.

✓ Before developing your plan, take time to **Reflect** and **Reload**.

✓ Good plans require two complementary approaches: **The Inside Route** and **The Outside Route.**

✓ Conduct **market research** so you can speak your client's language, understand their needs, and stay abreast of new industry trends and insights.

✓ **Identify** and focus on your top-tier customers. When you achieve success with them, others will follow.

✓ Focus on your **vertical** markets. When you become an industry expert, you can craft repeatable solutions that help you leapfrog the competition.

✓ **Where** we take our customers is the key to **driving their success**. We'll explore this in depth in chapter 4.

4

GUIDE YOUR CLIENTS TO SUCCESS

In 1963, Sherpa Nawang Gombu helped Jim Whittaker become the first American to reach the summit of Everest. *(Jim Whittaker)*

One of the best ways to persuade others is with your ears—by listening to them.

—Dean Rusk, U.S. secretary of state, 1961–1969

In 1984, Phil Ershler became the first American to summit Everest's North Face.
(Phil Ershler)

On the eve of his twenty-fourth birthday in 1986, John accepted an invitation to become the fourth member of a team planning their first climb of Mount Rainier. When he learned that the expedition would be guided by Phil Ershler, the first American to summit Mount Everest's North Face and the seventh person to conquer the Seven Summits, he was quick to accept.

Phil would share guiding duties with his close friend Nawang Gombu ("Gombu"), an acclaimed Sherpa guide and nephew of the great Tenzing Norgay, who, together with Sir Edmund Hillary, made history in 1953 as the first climbers to reach the summit of Everest. Gombu would later become the first person to conquer Everest twice: helping Jim Whittaker become the first American to reach the summit in 1963, and then guiding the first successful Indian expedition in 1965.

Although the four fledgling climbers were new to Rainier, they felt excited and confident about their prospects. They knew they were in very good hands.

Phil and Gombu helped the team master the skills they would need to reach the summit and return safely. They taught them how to walk uphill properly, breathing with each step to oxygenate their fatigued muscles. They showed them how to work with ropes, crampons, and ice axes. They also instilled a sense of teamwork and shared purpose, emphasizing the importance of supporting and listening to one another as they scaled the icy, glaciated mountain. In short, Phil and Gombu were exceptional leaders and guides: patient, insightful, and strong. Thanks to them, the expedition was a success.

Afterward, the team gathered at the historic Paradise Lodge in Mount Rainier National Park to celebrate their accomplishment. John fell into casual conversation with the lead climber from a second Rainier team, who shared his recent experiences attempting—but failing—to reach the summit of Everest. John was mesmerized by the man's Himalayan exploits and deeply impressed by his determination to return one day and succeed. He never caught the climber's name, but almost fifteen years later, fate would bring them together once more on the slopes of Everest.

The Rainier climb would prove to be a life-changing event for more than just John. Five years later his close friend, Sue, would meet and marry Phil. Together with their mutual friend, Andy Lufkin, the four would pursue a shared dream to climb the Seven Summits together. By 2000, they had nearly fulfilled their quest. With Phil serving as their guide, Sue, John, and Andy felt ready to climb Everest the following spring. They were confident they had the perfect team to confront their final challenge and succeed.

On the mountain, trust is everything. Team members depend on one another for their very survival. So the group was concerned, and somewhat deflated, when Andy informed them he wouldn't be joining them after all. He and his wife, Vivian, were expecting their first child. Although Everest still beckoned, Andy had new priorities and a new vision to fulfill.

With less than six months to go, the team was down to only three climbers. Once again, Phil demonstrated his leadership by reaching out to Charlie Peck, an experienced climber with the necessary skills and conditioning. John and Sue initially expressed reservations about relying on someone they had never met as they faced the greatest climbing challenge of their lives. But they trusted Phil's judgment and were pleased when Charlie accepted.

However, Phil had yet another critical decision to make. Almost two decades had passed since his last Everest climb. During these years, he had battled and overcome serious health issues. Although he now felt strong, Phil had the insight and experience to recognize that he might not be fully prepared to lead the team safely without the assistance of another experienced guide. He shared these concerns with Sue and John, and once again, they placed their trust in him to make the right decision for the team and the expedition.

Phil reached out to Greg Wilson, who had successfully guided climbers up the Southeast Ridge route they would be taking four times in the last five years. The two men had climbed together many times and developed a strong bond of mutual respect. Phil trusted Greg and knew that they could work together as fellow guides, just as Phil and Gombu had fifteen years before on Rainier.

In March 2001, Phil, John, Sue, and Charlie flew to Kathmandu, where they found Greg waiting for them, surrounded by dozens of duffel bags filled with gear and supplies. As they shook hands, John had an odd sense of déjà vu. He felt strongly that he had met Greg before in another time and place. Then, suddenly, it came to him. Greg was the lead climber he had met at the Paradise Lodge after summiting Rainier. Fate had brought them together, fifteen years and half a world away, to achieve their Everest vision together.

Think Like a Guide, Not Like a Salesperson

On the mountain, a skilled guide can spell the difference between life and death. In the field, you can make a similar impact on your client and his business by learning to think like a guide, not like a salesperson. But first you must cultivate the skills and expertise required to earn your client's trust and convince them to "clip into your rope." Only then can you guide them to success.

As a guide, you'll discover that success in business—as on the mountain—is something you and your client can achieve together. This is the surest path to reaping the personal rewards and professional recognition earned by top performers. But what exactly is a guide and how can *you* become one?

In sales, a guide is a wise and trusted teacher who brings deep experience and business insights to the client's needs and organizational challenges. You may be surprised to learn that we've been helping you develop the skills and habits of a guide since the beginning of this book!

- In chapters 1 and 2, you learned to Project your vision and to Travel Light. You also acquired the planning skills needed to achieve your goals, step by step, by Working Backward.

- Next, in chapter 3, you began to Prepare for success by Reflecting and Reloading, a rigorous process of self-evaluation and personal goal-setting that allows you to improve your performance on an ongoing basis. You also started to travel the Inside Route, developing the in-depth knowledge needed to present your company, products, and services with authority and confidence.

> Finally, you began to explore the **Who, What,** *and* **Where**—the **three Ws**—that define the Outside Route, where you meet with clients and close business.

In this chapter, we'll revisit the Outside Route and provide fresh perspectives about the skills and expertise you'll need to become your client's trusted guide. We'll consider the most dangerous pitfalls to avoid along this path. Most important, we'll learn how a guide determines **Where** to take their client and how this destination becomes a win/win for all concerned.

The Outside Route *Revisited*

As we've learned, your journey through the Outside Route is framed by the **three Ws: Who, What,** and **Where.** This three-part planning process is designed to help you acquire deep knowledge about your prospects and to develop the business insights needed to provide them with compelling solutions.

In the **Who** phase, we spotlighted Market Plans as the means to educate yourself about the companies in your territory, the products and services they sell, the markets in which they compete, and the key decision makers and influencers you must target to win a sale.

In recent years, this targeting process has become much more challenging because of a growing trend toward consensus purchasing. Whereas in the past, purchasing decisions were made behind closed doors by a single individual or a small team of senior executives, today purchasing is a more transparent process involving stakeholders across the entire organization. This means that you must first identify and then build relationships with every one of these individuals to be successful. We'll reflect this new reality when we begin to refine your Account Plan.

But first, stop and congratulate yourself. Thanks to the lessons of chapter 3, you're now an expert on your company and everything it has to offer. You've expanded the scope of this expertise to encompass your client's industry and markets. You may feel that you know their business better than they do. You might even be right!

Be careful, though. You're facing your first serious pitfall. It's not yet time to dazzle the prospect by proposing a slew of compelling new business solutions and improvements. It's time to *listen*.

> *Cerro Aconcagua ("Aconcagua") is located in the Andes mountain range about seventy miles northwest of Mendoza, the capital city of Argentina's Mendoza province. At 22,841 feet, it's the highest mountain in the Americas. It's also one of the most deceptive and deadly of the Seven Summits, claiming multiple casualties every year.*
>
> *The first two thirds of the mountain are composed of dirt,*

Cerro Aconcagua. *(Phil Ershler)*

scree, and rock, which an experienced climber can navigate with relative ease. But when they reach High Camp at about 18,000 feet, climbers discover a very different and far more daunting Aconcagua. At these high altitudes, the mountain is extremely treacherous and dangerous. On Summit Day, climbers must ask themselves if they have the energy and reserves to complete the nearly 5,000-foot vertical climb up steep flanks covered with splintered glaciers and ice. As Phil puts it, "Aconcagua looks best in your rearview mirror."

Nevertheless, in 1997 Phil agreed to lead an expedition to Aconcagua, guiding John, Andy, and two friends, Mike and Mark, who had little experience with high-altitude climbs. After careful consideration, Phil selected the Polish Glacier Traverse route, which is also known as the "Falso de los Polacos."

The climb went well for the first week, with all of the climbers feeling strong and working well together. But as the altitude increased, it became clear that Mark was struggling to adapt to the thinning air. Phil knew that some people acclimate more quickly than others, so he showed Mark how to breathe properly, pace himself, and preserve his energy for Summit Day. Thanks to Phil, everyone reached High Camp safely.

At this point, Phil carefully considered his next steps. He knew that it takes months of planning and preparation to climb a challenging mountain like Aconcagua. Failing was never contemplated. Climbers see summits, not failure. So they may overestimate their capabilities and ignore clear signs that they are not yet ready to achieve their summit dream. Guides also understand that reaching the summit is only half the journey. Success requires a safe round-trip trek from the base to the summit and back again. So they carefully evaluate the weather and terrain, as well as each climber's conditioning, ability, and readiness to succeed.

Phil knew that the weather was deteriorating and that he

could risk only one attempt to reach the summit. The team would need to maintain a brisk pace if they hoped to return safely to High Camp before dark. After two weeks on the mountain, John, Andy, and Mike felt strong and fully prepared to summit that night. Mark was convinced he too was ready to proceed. But Phil thought otherwise.

Mark's pace had not improved over the past week. His mind and heart were sound and his positive attitude was inspiring to everyone. But Phil feared that Mark wouldn't be able to keep up when they reached the upper glacier, putting the entire team in danger. He asked to speak to Mark alone.

As always, Phil's approach was measured, analytical, and supportive. He began by asking Mark how he was feeling and how prepared he felt for the difficult and dangerous climbs ahead. Understandably, each question provoked an emotional response from Mark. But, thanks to the trust and mutual respect between them, Mark was able to answer with total candor and to accurately assess his likelihood of success. In the end, it was his decision—not Phil's—to let the team summit without him. Like all great guides, Phil helped Mark navigate his own route, undeterred by this temporary setback and eager to try again on another day and another mountain.

Listening to the "What"

In chapter 3, we described the Situation, Problem, Implication, and Need process that produces the information required to develop an effective Account Plan. We also noted the limitations of SPIN analysis, which can only *extract* problems that are already known and acknowledged by the client. In this chapter, we'll show you how an effective What analysis can do much more than this. It can provide the foundation for a long-lasting, trusting relationship.

When you meet with clients, encourage them to speak openly

about their challenges, needs, and concerns. Ask leading, open-ended questions that tease out every detail of every problem as well as their perceived implications. You can't earn your client's trust and serve as their guide without first knowing where *they* think they need to go. Listen and be patient. You'll soon get your chance to shine!

On the mountain, guides are masters of planning and preparation. The same is true in sales. Carefully map out all of your questions well in advance of the meeting. Make sure they address every individual's specific concerns, roles, and responsibilities. But don't stop there. Practice your questions so you can focus on listening, not speaking. Take careful notes. Make the meeting count.

Now it's time to refer back to our Account Plan chart from chapter 3. As you can see, we've refined this plan to reflect the essential importance of listening and the new reality of the consensus purchasing process.

The Account Plan *Refined* The **What**	<ul><li>A detailed company profile that includes divisions, subsidiaries, departments, markets, and competitors. If the company is public, also include a summary of the financials, risk factors, and other useful information disclosed in its SEC filings.</li><li>List and describe all of the company's systems, products, and services that are relevant to your sales campaign.</li><li>An expanded organizational chart that reflects *all* of the stakeholders participating in the consensus purchasing process.</li></ul>

The Account Plan *Refined*
The **What**

- Guide each of these stakeholders through a SPIN analysis by asking leading questions and *listening* carefully to everything they say.
- Create a solution designed to meet these Needs and a preliminary schedule to implement it.
- Maintain meeting schedules and track outcomes.

Crossing the Ice Bridge

You've demonstrated respect for your customer by listening carefully and acknowledging their perceptions. You've shown restraint in expressing your own ideas, although you were nearly ready to explode with proposed solutions! In doing so, you've developed the foundation for a solid relationship based on mutual trust. You've demonstrated the skills and attitudes needed to serve as a guide. Your client is now ready to "clip their rope to yours" and let you lead them across the Ice Bridge from the **What** to the **Where**.

Ice bridges are sections of an ice field that cover dangerous crevasses and allow passage across difficult terrain. As a guide, your job is now to help your client overcome these obstacles and achieve their vision and goals by sharing your hard-won insights and expertise.

Prior to crossing the Ice Bridge, all routes appear to be known. Your client may already have a specific solution in mind, based on the advice of a consultant or the influence of a competitor. They may even have a working knowledge of the products, services, and technologies offered by your company and its competitors.

If you accepted the client's assumptions and conclusions, you'd find yourself competing based on product comparisons and price alone. But top performers have the courage and confidence to challenge their clients' assumptions and guide them across the Ice

John and Greg navigating the Khumbu Icefall. *(Charlie Peck)*

Bridge to a superior solution, one that their company is uniquely positioned to provide.

Challenging the client does *not* mean rejecting their perceptions out of hand or blithely informing them that they are flat out wrong. It *does* mean changing the conversation and reframing their perceptions about the nature and extent of their business problems. Only then can you begin to cross the Ice Bridge together.

Revisit every problem your client has identified and begin sharing the expertise and insights you've acquired through your market research and experiences with other companies. Ask your client to consider the potential impact of new problems they may have overlooked. Make sure they've taken into account such factors as:

- Emerging and disruptive technologies

- New competitors they will soon encounter and their competitive strategies

- Relationships among key suppliers

- The potential impact of new laws and regulations

- Changing workforce demographics

- Finance and tax implications

- Pricing models and lifetime costs

The New Route

You've made great progress. Your clients have clipped their rope to yours and you've successfully led them across the Ice Bridge. They're engaged in a new conversation about their company, industry, and competitors. Now, at long last, it's time to start guiding them **Where** you believe they should go. This is the **New Route**: a path they never knew existed until you blazed the trail. The New Route:

- Solves the problems you reframed and reprioritized during the challenge process.

- Maps directly to your company's products and services.

- Creates new long-term business opportunities for you and your client.

- Helps your client achieve their own vision and goals.

While serving as CEO of Saltmine, Inc., a Web design and development firm located in Seattle, John made a point of spending time with each new client during their first business meeting. These conversations rarely focused on Saltmine's expertise, products, or services. Instead John encouraged the clients to share their overarching vision and goals. This was an essential first step in guiding his client to the New Route.

> One client told me he wanted to automate a labor-intensive manual process for his biggest customer, a buying group within Starbucks. The client was convinced this would save the group time and money when ordering specialty items while increasing his firm's margins on every transaction. He felt the best way to accomplish this would be for Saltmine to develop an enterprise-class supply-chain management application capable of accommodating all of the hundreds of buying groups within Starbucks. I knew that an application of this scope and complexity would cost more than a million dollars to design, develop, test, and deploy.
>
> From my Outside Route planning, I also knew that Starbucks was operationally dependent on an Enterprise Resource Planning infrastructure from a world leader in enterprise software, which already provided many of the features the client was asking us to duplicate. It was extremely unlikely that many Starbucks departments would willingly abandon an established application from a global supply chain software leader in favor of a new, untried application offered by my client.
>
> But I wanted my client to achieve his vision of expanding his Starbucks business. So instead of focusing on making the largest sale possible, I challenged his perceptions about this Need by sharing my business insights and expertise. Together we conceived a new multistage Account Plan. For $50,000, Saltmine would develop a modest application that met my client's initial goals of streamlining operations for his current Starbucks purchasing group. Then, once the application had proven its worth, Saltmine would develop new software components to accommodate additional buying groups as they came on board.

The results were outstanding. The buying group was delighted with the new application and shared glowing reviews with other Starbucks departments. Slowly and organically, the client began to expand its presence within Starbucks, awarding my firm a string of lucrative development contracts that eventually generated as much revenue as the ambitious application the client had originally envisioned. It was a classic win/win. With my help and guidance, Saltmine and the client crossed the Ice Bridge together.

The Confident Route

Top performers know they must chart out the New Route very carefully. They understand that it's not enough to simply define a compelling value proposition (a process that we'll explore fully in a later chapter). They recognize that there are many routes up every mountain and many ways to meet the evolving needs of their clients.

The Inside Route armed you with a comprehensive knowledge of your company, products, and services. You take pride in its strengths and fully recognize its weaknesses. You must now take these into account as you begin to chart the New Route.

Your New Route should link the needs you identified and reframed after challenging the client to a tailored set of products and services that only your company can provide. This means that you must have total confidence in your company's ability to perform and deliver. In other words, the New Route must also be the **Confident Route**! Otherwise, all of your time, effort, and expertise will come to nothing.

Make sure your client understands what the New Route is and how it will meet their vision and goals. Explain why you are taking them in this new direction by discussing —and dismissing —alternative routes. Emphasize your company's unique strengths. If there are weaknesses, address them forthrightly and demonstrate how you plan to overcome them. If you do this, the Confident Route will be a sure path to earning the recognition and rewards of a top performer.

Xerox Corporation is renowned for its development of the first graphical user interface, which led to the launch of such market-leading software companies as Apple and Microsoft. But in the mid-1980s, Xerox was at a crossroads when Japanese competitors stealthily developed the next breakthrough in copy technology: color copies. Suddenly, tons of shiny new products arrived en masse on American shores. The once-untouchable company found itself losing business and market share at an unprecedented rate.

One of Xerox's sales management leaders at the time was District Sales Manager Jay Tyler, who operated out of the company's Seattle office. Jay watched in dismay as each of his customers and prospects was approached by his color copier competitors. Like all true leaders and guides, he decided to confront the new market reality head-on and find a new way to win.

Although Xerox could no longer compete on the basis of superior technology, the company still boasted the best sales force in the world and a top-notch service organization. So Jay resolved to succeed by guiding the sales process to fully exploit these organizational strengths while minimizing the impact of the company's technological weaknesses. He invited John and several other young sales representatives to participate in a presentation he had scheduled with the Boeing Company, the branch's single biggest customer.

After introductions and pleasantries were exchanged, Jay silently approached the front of the room and turned out all the lights. Then, in the pitch-black room, Jay loudly and confidently proclaimed, "Xerox does not make color copiers!" The room exploded with laughter. Jay went on to explain that Xerox was working on color technology, which was true. He also acknowledged that the Japanese products were capable of making beautiful color copies during the short course of a sales presentation.

However, he added, the color technology they were using was not yet stable. After a few months of commercial use, the toner colors would begin to mix and the brilliant colors would degrade into dull browns. When that happened, Boeing would not just have inferior copies. They'd also have to contend with the nightmare of securing replacement parts and arranging service calls from an overseas company with a vastly inferior support organization.

As the market leader, Jay said, Xerox would never offer flashy technology at the expense of quality. The company wouldn't introduce its own color copiers until they were as solid and reliable as their black-and-white counterparts. And they would back this quality commitment with a service and support organization that was universally acknowledged to be the best in the industry.

The entire tenor of the meeting changed from that point on. Jay had challenged his clients, guiding them to a Confident Route and then leading them across the Ice Bridge. Boeing would remain a Xerox client and business partner for many years to come. And when Xerox later fulfilled its promise to introduce mature color technology, it would regain much of the market share it had lost to its first-mover competitors.

So we've now made tremendous progress toward achieving our goal of becoming our client's trusted advisor and guide. We've learned to challenge the client after building a solid foundation for a long-term, mutually beneficial relationship. We've blazed a Confident Route and crossed the Ice Bridge connecting the **What** to the **Where**. Now, let's incorporate what we've learned into the final version of our Account Plan chart.

The Account Plan *Finalized*
Navigating from the
What to the **Where**

- A detailed company profile that includes divisions, subsidiaries, departments, markets, and competitors. If the company is public, also include a summary of the financials, risk factors, and other useful information disclosed in its SEC filings.

- List and describe all of the company's systems, products, and services that are relevant to your sales campaign.

- Maintain meeting schedules and track outcomes.

- An expanded organizational chart that reflects *all* of the stakeholders participating in the consensus purchasing process.

- Guide each of these stakeholders through a SPIN analysis by asking leading questions and *listening* carefully to everything they say.

- Challenge the customer and share your insights to reframe their business Problems and Implications.

- Define a New/Confident Route that meets your client's new Needs and a preliminary schedule to traverse it.

- Cross the Ice Bridge together.

We'll complete our examination of the **Where** process later in this book, when we explain how to craft the specific solution that will enable you and your client to cross the Ice Bridge together. For now, take pride in having advanced from salesperson to guide. You're becoming a trusted advisor, providing your client with new insights and helping them navigate new routes to business success. In turn, they're making it possible for you to secure the financial rewards and career recognition that accrue to top performers.

But be careful to avoid the pitfalls of arrogance and complacency. Becoming a guide is just the first step in a never-ending process. Guides continuously challenge themselves to develop their craft and perfect their expertise. They're humble. They know they must always *listen* to their clients before they can *teach* them.

> On April 29, 2001, John and Sue noticed a young Sherpa smiling at them as they passed on their way to Mount Everest's Camp II. "That's Babu Chiri, the legendary Sherpa guide," Phil told them. Babu had reached the summit of Everest ten times and held two world records: one for making the fastest ascent of Everest—in just sixteen hours and fifty-six minutes; and another for spending twenty-one hours at the summit without supplemental oxygen.
>
> The next morning, they were awakened by the sound of frantic voices blaring through Phil's guide radio. Babu had fallen to his death through a snow bridge into a deep crevasse. They were hearing the rescue team of three climbers struggling to retrieve his lifeless body so it could be transported down the mountain to Kathmandu.
>
> Babu's untimely death shocked and paralyzed everyone at Camp II. "What are we doing here?" John and Sue asked themselves. They assumed their Sherpa teams would be too grief-stricken to continue, spelling the end of their hopes to reach the summit that year. Perhaps this was for the best, they told them-

selves, mourning the passing of a great climber, who transcended humble beginnings to become a world-class guide, environmentalist, business owner, and humanitarian.

But Sherpas have a more philosophical attitude about death than do most Westerners. In the Sherpa view, Babu had gone to a better place, or, as his brother Dawa so eloquently put it, "Babu has gone to Tibet." Babu's death became an opportunity to celebrate the inspiring life of a great man and his singular achievements.

John and Sue felt mixed emotions when Phil told them the expedition would continue. On the one hand, they were pleased to have another chance to summit Everest. On the other, they felt frightened and uneasy. If an experienced guide and mountaineer like Babu could die on the mountain, what assurances did they have that the same fate wouldn't befall them?

As always, Phil was there to offer firm guidance and support. "Babu's death was a tragic accident, a fluke," he told them. "We all feel terrible about it. But it doesn't change anything for us. This mountain is no more dangerous today than it was yesterday. If we want to honor his memory, we should focus on accomplishing what we set out to do."

The team trusted Phil and the knowledge and expertise he'd accumulated during his thirty-five-year career as a climber and guide. So the following morning, they continued up the mountain, climbing step by step, inch by inch, on their quest to reach the top of the world.

In this chapter, we took a closer look at the Outside Route and how it prepares us to guide our clients to success. We expanded the scope of our SPIN analysis to encompass every member of our client's consensus purchasing team. We learned how to listen to our customers and challenge their preconceived assumptions. Our enhanced understanding of the **Who, What**, and **Where** empowered us to guide them on a new and confident route across the Ice Bridge.

No one starts out as a guide. It takes dedication, hard work, resilience, and the humility to listen before we speak. Guides emulate the leaders who inspired *them* and helped them grow: people like Nawang Gombu, Jay Tyler, Babu Chiri, and Phil Ershler. By now, you've probably realized something about this book and its authors too. Our goal is to pass on the lessons we learned in the field and on the mountain. In this way, we hope to guide you to a new plateau of sales success—one you may never have imagined you could reach. Here are the key takeaways from this chapter:

✓ To become a top performer, **think like a guide**, not a salesperson.

✓ Revisit the **Three Ws**, with particular emphasis on the **What**, by listening carefully to your customers' perspectives on their problems, needs, and goals. Be humble.

✓ Commit yourself to helping your clients achieve their vision and goals. This is the key to developing strong, **trusting client relationships**.

✓ **Challenge** your clients and reframe their perspectives by **sharing your insights**.

✓ Define a **New/Confident Route** and then lead your client across the **Ice Bridge**. If you lead your customers to success, you will be successful too.

5

BUILD YOUR SHERPA TEAM

Sue and team—Mount Vinson. *(Phil Ershler)*

We don't climb mountains alone!

To get the full value of joy you must have somebody to divide it with.

—*Mark Twain*

Vinson Massif, located in the Sentinel Range of the Ellsworth Mountains, is the highest mountain in Antarctica. Towering 16,050 feet above sea level, it is so remote and forbidding that it wasn't climbed successfully until 1966.

There are only three reasons to go to Antarctica: to touch the South Pole; to view the four-foot-tall emperor penguins the region is known for; and for Seven Summit climbers, to reach the peak of Mount Vinson. The tourist route to Antarctica usually presents little, if any, danger. But climbing Vinson is a different story. Although it isn't the highest of the Seven Summits, it is indisputably among the most dangerous, challenging climbers with punishing weather and temperatures that hover near 20°F.

There are no airstrips in the region, so John flew onto the rugged ice of Antarctica on a Lockheed C-130 Hercules, a four-engine turboprop military transport aircraft. Landing at Patriot Hills, the plane slid for more than six miles before coming to a stop. After another short flight on a Twin Otter to Vinson Base Camp, his team donned their packs and began to climb, dragging sleds loaded with their tents, supplies, and climbing gear.

Conditions like these can quickly sap a climber's strength, making a 16,000-foot climb feel like 26,000 feet. After each grueling day, the team made camp by cutting ice into large blocks to form a windbreak that would prevent their tents from being blown over during the night and help minimize the impact of the windchill.

Finally, after a week of intense effort, John and his team successfully summited Vinson. But their challenges were far from over. When they returned to Patriot Hills, they learned that the aircraft they had counted on to retrieve them would be unable to land due to the eroding weather conditions. They were stranded, along with several other climbing teams and tourist groups.

They were a larger team now, with a new collective goal: survival! Days, and then weeks, passed with no sign that the weather was improving enough for their rescue plane to land. The food supply started to run low, so members of the various teams began working together to devise strategies to ration food and maintain the igloolike walls they depended upon to protect them from the

*penetrating cold. To maintain their morale, they chatted, played
trivia games, shared stories, and told jokes. Sometimes they were
so bored they found themselves counting the fabric squares that
formed the walls of their tents.*

*Finally, blessedly, they heard the roar of approaching turbo-
prop engines and saw a huge transport aircraft dip below the
clouds and thunder down onto the ice. With gratitude and relief,
they congratulated one another for the teamwork that helped
them make it through together.*

Don't Be a Soloist

Imagine facing a situation like this alone. Without help, could you
excavate and assemble a windbreak of ice blocks while the wind
howled around you? Would you be able to sustain your confidence
and strength after weeks of uncertainty, hunger, and isolation? It's
no accident that climbing is typically a team activity. On the mountain, as in business, teams outperform individuals.

Of course, there are many climbers who would scoff at the notion that a mountain, even one as forbidding as Vinson Massif, can't
be climbed alone. They're right. Throughout history, lone wolves
have achieved remarkable feats. An Austrian climber, for example,
climbed all of the Seven Summits alone without stopping at inter-
mediate camps or using supplementary oxygen.

For most climbers, however, going it alone is neither the safest
nor the most efficient way to reach the summit. Inevitably, soloists
run smack up against the limits of what they can achieve on their
own. Without the support and experience of a team, they can expose
themselves to extreme risks that reduce their chances of a successful
outcome.

In sales, too, lone wolves can leave themselves vulnerable when they fail to forge the long-term relationships, teams, and networks they need to achieve at the highest levels throughout their careers. They may find intermittent success thanks to their great instincts, confidence, and drive to achieve. But these attributes will only serve them well for a while. Inevitably they will experience a major setback, such as a lost sale caused by their failure to consult with colleagues to confirm the technical feasibility of a proposed solution.

Top sales performers refuse to be stymied by their personal limitations. They set lofty goals and find ways to achieve them on an ongoing basis. Because they recognize that they must rely on others, they establish partnerships with influential members of their civic and business communities to acquire industry knowledge and client access. They invest in building strong relationships with their company's leaders to secure the organizational resources they need to mount successful sales campaigns. Then they leverage these relationships to recruit and lead cross-functional teams to the summit of sales success.

After reading the first four chapters of this book, you may have come to the conclusion that our goal is to groom you to become a solo performer. Not so! The skills you've been developing will certainly help you become a successful salesperson: a Competent Climber. However, our goal for you is much more ambitious. We want you to achieve your full potential as a *top performer*!

On Everest, climbers rely on Sherpas to help them reach the summit. In this chapter, we'll show you how to build and lead your own "Sherpa sales team." In the process, you'll advance from Competent Climber to Team Leader; the next stage in your ascent to top performer status.

Why Are Teams Important?

As we discussed in chapter 4, elite sales performers help their clients succeed by guiding them across the Ice Bridge and blazing a confident trail to business solutions their company is uniquely positioned to deliver. By their very nature, these solutions can be quite complex, spanning multiple technologies, business processes, and areas of expertise. They may cost tens of millions of dollars or more and be implemented in stages over several years, requiring complicated financing arrangements, stringent project management, and the willing cooperation of multiple departments over the course of a sales contract.

Recognizing this, companies are placing growing importance on interdepartmental collaboration, reaching across traditional operational silos to deploy flexible cross-functional teams. From the sales perspective, this offers many practical benefits:

- **Safety in Numbers.** Let's face it, sales calls can be stressful! It's hard to stay confident and focused when your PowerPoint misbehaves or you draw a blank at a crucial moment. A well-chosen team will help you get back on track quickly and seamlessly.

- **Demonstrating Expertise**. Carefully consider who will be attending the meeting on the client side. Is the finance department represented? Will someone from information technology be participating? Make sure your team includes individuals who possess the corresponding skills and expertise. This will allow you to demonstrate the depth of your firm's capabilities while introducing the key players your client will collaborate with if you close the deal.

- **Oversight Safety Net**. In the heat of the meeting, you may forget to communicate a key point or miss the significance of a client's passing comment or question. When this happens, your team can serve as a real-time sounding board, shifting the focus back to your message and spotlighting the meaning and significance of the client's feedback, afterward during the postmeeting debrief.

- **Mentorship**. We all have room for improvement. From time to time, consider inviting a more senior-level sales executive to accompany you to an important meeting. They can provide insights and constructive criticism that will be invaluable to your professional development and help you advance your sales campaign.

At Everest Base Camp, Sue fell into conversation with a fellow climber who was about to make his fifth attempt to reach the summit alone. Although his previous four attempts had failed, he was determined to accept no help or support of any kind as he made his way through the treacherous Khumbu Icefall and onward to the upper flanks of the mountain.

Sue expressed encouragement and wished him luck. But privately she wondered why anyone would choose such a lonely path to success. Even if he did summit this time, no one would be there to share the achievement and celebrate with him.

A week later, Sue encountered the climber again, this time camping alone at Camp III on the Lhotse Face. She stopped by his tent to offer a cup of tea and an energy bar. He responded that while he appreciated her kind offer, he couldn't accept it because he hadn't carried the items there himself.

As a soloist, he had severely limited his chances for success. Ultimately, he would fail again.

When Teams Unravel

Teams require constant attention. In business, teammates who don't pull their weight can be coached, motivated, or placed in alternative capacities that better suit their skills and temperaments. In climbing, there's much less flexibility. One person's failure can put everyone in danger.

Lhotse is the fourth-highest mountain in the world and closely connected to Everest. Both mountains share a common route for the first 25,000 feet. After that, the routes diverge to their respective peaks.

In May 2001, a group of three British climbers began their descent from Lhotse's summit. Exhausted and disoriented from their climb, they allowed themselves to be separated. One of them, a nineteen-year-old climber, was so tired that he tried to hasten his descent by removing his clip from the safety rope. Moments later, he lost his footing and plunged over 1,500 feet. Miraculously, he was able to reach out with his ice ax and arrest his fall, landing on a near-vertical perch located on the shared route between Camps III and IV on the Lhotse Face.

As he sat dazed and alone on the ice, climbing teams from around the world began to communicate by radio, urgently searching for a way to save his life. From their vantage point far below at Camp II, Sue and John could see the fallen climber and hear the rapid-fire radio communications among Phil and his fellow guides. Everyone agreed that the teams at Camp II and Camp III were simply too far away to execute a timely rescue. So Phil radioed the only teams that could possibly help—climbers poised at the High Camps on Everest and Lhotse, where they were resting in preparation for their push to the summit the following night.

Phil knew that he was asking a great deal. It was unlikely that these climbers could rescue the young climber and then return to camp with sufficient energy to achieve their summit dream. Unless one of them was willing to put his personal ambitions on hold, the British climber was going to die.

Simone Moro and Denis Urubko were at Lhotse High Camp, preparing to summit, when the fallen climber's teammates arrived and begged for help. Generously, Moro accepted the challenge and went searching for the climber. Finally, as the sun rose, *he found him, battered and half-frozen, without gloves, head-lamp, and, worse, the crampons that would allow him to climb the icy slope. In Moro's words, "He told me to go away and leave him to die. In Italian dialect, I told him that after having made such an effort to reach him, I'd even carry him piggyback. And that's what I did."*

Thanks to Moro's heroism, the British climber survived. But the extreme effort he devoted to the rescue totally drained his energy reserves. Moro would not reach Lhotse's summit that year.

The British climber's team had failed in its most important mission: to ensure that everyone returned safely to camp. But, thanks to the teamwork shown by the Lhotse and Everest climbers, his life was saved. In sales, as on the mountain, major opportunities can pose unexpected risks that may lead to sudden disaster. On those occasions, a team can make the difference between success and failure.

Building Your Sherpa Sales Team

A well-constructed Sherpa sales team will provide the knowledge, experience, and resources you need to lead a sales campaign to its successful conclusion. Each of the team members should also possess the key personality traits that can help make *any* team successful. We'll use the acronym ROPE to illustrate some of the most important attributes.

R	Reliable	R	Responsible	?	What other team attributes do you think are important?
O	Opportunity-driven	O	Organized	?	
P	Professional	P	Practical	?	
E	Enthusiastic	E	Expert	?	

As with the Inside and Outside routes, there are two types of Sherpa sales teams:

- Your *Inside* ROPE team is drawn from within your company. It may include key members from virtually every department.

- Your *Outside* ROPE team is drawn from the community at large. It should provide access to decision makers, industry experts, and other resources that can offer you a competitive advantage.

In sports, teams deploy scouts to help them identify and recruit the most talented players. Top sales performers take the same approach in building *their* teams.

Building Your Inside ROPE Team

Let's start with your Inside ROPE team. In chapter 3, we showed you how to develop an in-depth understanding of your company, products, services, and markets. But if you're like many salespeople, you may have devoted too little attention to building your organizational chart and documenting each department's roles and responsibilities.

All too often, salespeople take a dismissive attitude toward their peers in other departments. According to a common refrain, "If it weren't for sales, accounting wouldn't have anything to account for!" However, you can't scout for the most talented team members if you don't value what they do or understand the potential contributions they can make to your sales campaigns.

Consider the following chart:

✓ Department	✓ Roles/Potential Contributions to the Sales Campaign
✓ Engineering	✓ Converting functional requirements into system designs, drawings, and specifications.
✓ Finance	✓ Completing the financial sections of large proposals, ensuring that deals are profitable.
✓ Human Resources	✓ Determining staffing requirements and setting realistic time frames for delivering your solutions.
✓ Legal	✓ Negotiating and monitoring sales contracts.
✓ Management	✓ Setting company strategy, developing organizational capacity, allocating company resources, mentoring, and helping to secure the support of your client's senior executives.
✓ Manufacturing	✓ Ensuring that the systems designed by Engineering can be correctly built and delivered on time.
✓ Marketing	✓ Identifying and analyzing market trends, revenue opportunities, and competitive positioning.
✓ Operations	✓ Implementing and maintaining solutions and providing customer and technical support.
✓ Product Management	✓ Defining products, features, pricing, integration capabilities, and release schedules.
✓ Sales	✓ The top performers in your department possess great wisdom and experience. If you reach out and build relationships with them, they will help you succeed.
✓ Technology	✓ Performing research and development, anticipating, and responding to technology trends.

Crossing Company Crevasses

Companies are like mountains, with deep crevasses between departments that make it difficult for them to collaborate. Top sales performers *cross these crevasses* by educating themselves and making at least one friend in every organizational unit. They understand that almost every department has something to contribute, whether it's by serving as internal influencers and/or decision makers or by providing essential resources at critical points during the sales process.

Begin now by reaching out across departments to cultivate the relationships you may need in the future. Get to know the most talented and productive employees in your company. Don't ignore your own department! The top performers there can help you improve your skills while providing you with key selling insights.

Treat your Inside ROPE team candidates like potential clients. Find out what motivates them and help them succeed. Get together socially over lunch or dinner. When the time comes, they'll repay you in spades.

Remember too that cross-departmental teams are not built overnight. It takes time and planning to cross the crevasses. Start by setting clearly defined team-building goals during your Reflect and Reload process and then carefully track your performance. If your team-building skills are deficient, acknowledge this during your annual Inside Route self-assessment and find concrete ways to improve them.

Competing for Company Resources

As we've seen, the most lucrative sales opportunities require the willing cooperation of multiple departments. But in most companies today, employees are being pressured to do more with less.

When resources are scarce and potential team members are over-burdened, what can top performers do to secure the support they need to succeed?

It all comes down to effective communications. As a peak per-former, it's your responsibility to keep the entire organization in-formed about the strategic sales opportunities you're pursuing and their importance to the business. Become an evangelist, sharing your enthusiasm and inspiring others to join your team and share the glory.

Recognize every important contribution made by another depart-ment. Keep executive management informed every step of the way. The momentum you build will sweep away any organizational ob-stacles standing in your way. When you win the business, everyone on your Inside ROPE team will stand at the summit with you.

Sue put this lesson to good use while she was climbing the cor-porate ladder in telecommunications, where she led a Seattle-based team responsible for selling nationwide data networks to her firm's largest and most strategic accounts. Several of these deals generated more than $100 million in revenue.

> I knew that huge opportunities like these can pose significant or-ganizational risks by taking resources away from smaller deals, de-railing the bread-and-butter sales that companies depend on year in and year out to keep them afloat and profitable. I recognized that it would be necessary for me to win the confidence and support of my executive team if I hoped to secure the resources I needed to pursue these strategic, high-risk/high-reward opportunities.
>
> So I made a point of making frequent visits to the company's corporate headquarters in Denver. There I met with the executive team, as well as with leaders from sales, finance, engineering, product marketing, and other departments to keep them informed about my progress with these major opportunities. In each case, I shared the client requirements I had identified, the key features of

the proposed solutions, the market insights I had gained, and the potential return on the company's investment. I also sought out their expertise and advice, treating them as highly valued members of my sales team. Between visits, I maintained the flow of information and recognized everyone's contributions via periodic e-mails and phone calls.

Thanks to these efforts, my team and I secured the cooperation and resources we needed to continue closing huge deals and earning the rewards and recognition of top performers.

Leading the Charge

You've identified a strategic sales opportunity, secured management buy-in, and scheduled an important client meeting. Now it's time to assemble the Inside ROPE team that will provide the precise mix of expertise and skills you need to achieve your meeting objectives. As team leader, it's also your responsibility to "think like a CEO" and orchestrate everyone's contributions to ensure the meeting proceeds smoothly and professionally.

- *Create a Meeting Agenda*. Your clients are busy people. They need to know how the meeting will address their needs and concerns. Your agenda should list the topics you'll be discussing and the names of each presenter. Your client may have additional topics they want to address, so be flexible!

- *Anticipate Questions*. Meet with each team member in advance to identify questions that may be directed at them during the meeting and the best ways to answer them.

- *Call the Plays*. Introduce every member of your team. Explain why they're participating and how they fit into the meeting agenda.

Then, serving as the head guide, lead the discussion and hand off relevant questions and topics to your team as appropriate.

- **Resolve Disputes**. Intervene promptly if your team members start to contradict or interrupt each other. You're responsible for ensuring that your team speaks with one voice and delivers a clear and consistent message.

- **Maintain Momentum**. After the meeting, thank each team member for their contributions. Review the high and low points. Ask for constructive feedback. Most importantly, make sure that every commitment your team made during the meeting has been identified and properly assigned. Then, while the meeting is still fresh in everyone's mind, contact the client to thank them for their time and recap the action items/next steps in the sales process.

With such clear and obvious benefits, you might wonder why *any* rational sales executive would prefer to work alone. Yet, surprisingly, some do. These are the "lone wolves," so called because they are typically so confident in their own abilities that they feel no need for guidance, management, alliances, or company resources. Lone wolves conduct their personal and professional lives in exactly the same way: outside of the pack, placing self-determination and personal achievement above everything else, marching to the beat of their own drummer. They may possess the talent and determination to excel for a time. But, lacking identity, support, and allegiance within the organization, most of them will ultimately be forced to move on.

Of course, lone wolves do have reasons for preferring to go solo. And some of them are good ones. They may have learned from hard experience that walking into a meeting with the wrong team can be a surefire recipe for disaster. Perhaps they were embarrassed by team members who scuttled a deal because they were unprepared or acquitted themselves poorly. Failures like these inevitably drove them away from the pack, squandering their talents and hindering their long-term success.

John still recalls with some embarrassment a high-profile meeting he arranged to present Verizon's wide-area data networking solutions to a new division at Microsoft.

> Determined to ensure that my troops could address any conceivable topic, I assembled a large team from across the company. But when everyone arrived, I discovered that my Verizon team outnumbered our Microsoft hosts by a two-to-one margin.
>
> Moments into the meeting, a Microsoft executive interrupted us and asked me to explain each team member's role in fulfilling the agenda. In truth, most of them were along simply for moral support in case I was blindsided by an unexpected question. When I acknowledged this, the executive asked all of the extraneous Verizon employees to leave. Not surprisingly, the meeting didn't go well. But I had learned a valuable lesson I would never forget.

As you assemble your Inside ROPE team, make sure that every member has a clear and specific role. It's your team, so build one that makes you proud!

Select individuals you are certain will add value. If you have several options, choose people with complementary personalities who enjoy working together. This will enhance the cohesiveness of the group and add to the enjoyment of the entire sales experience. The positive energy your team projects can be a powerful force in winning over your client and convincing them that your company is the right partner for their business.

Building Your Outside ROPE Team Through Networking

In chapter 3, we demonstrated how creating a Market Plan on the Outside Route helps you acquire industry expertise by identifying the key players, trends, prospects, and technologies driving your market opportunity. Now it's time to leverage this knowledge by reaching *outside* your company for allies who can help you find and close business. It's time to build your **Outside ROPE team** through *networking*.

Networking is simply an extension of what you've been doing all along: forging mutually beneficial relationships. The process is the same as the one you employed earlier to cross company crevasses. First, you'll need to scout out the best candidates. Then you must demonstrate a genuine commitment to helping them achieve their own goals and objectives. As always, this takes discipline, focus, and planning.

Let's begin by exploring **where** to find potential members of your *Outside* ROPE team. We've listed some of the best networking settings in the chart below:

✓ Networking Setting	✓ Networking Opportunity
✓ Industry Conferences	✓ Presents the most targeted group of potential additions to your network. You're all in the same industry and have many common interests. Even competitors can become trusted allies in certain circumstances—don't dismiss them!
✓ Chambers of Commerce	✓ Can be an excellent source of information about local businesses, providing you with immediate access to the people who run them. This is the best place to start entering a new region or territory.

✓ Networking Setting	✓ Networking Opportunity
✓ Business Networking Groups	✓ These groups typically regulate the number of people who can attend their meetings from a particular industry. So it's worth investing time to build relationships with the organizers so you can become the "go to" participant from your industry.
✓ Social Networking	✓ Social media sites like Facebook and LinkedIn can help you rapidly assemble a business network spanning hundreds of contacts. However, real relationships are built over time through shared experiences that promote mutual trust. So be sure to balance your online networking with face-to-face interactions.
✓ Lectures and Forums	✓ Help you broaden your knowledge about your industry and the key trends driving your business. Your instructors and fellow students may also be excellent candidates for your Outside ROPE team.
✓ Conventions	✓ At large gatherings, it can be difficult to zero in on the best candidates. So plan ahead by reviewing the convention schedule to see if you can arrange brief meetings with industry experts and presenters you admire. Since attendees may come from across the globe, conventions also provide a great opportunity to spend face time with candidates you might only see occasionally. And check out those badges! You never know whom you might stumble into or meet on the lunch line.
✓ Social Events	✓ Provide informal and potentially valuable opportunities to meet people who can help your business. Whether you're attending a Little League game, shooting eighteen holes, or simply relaxing at a bar or restaurant, make sure that everyone knows what you do. Remember, sales is—first and foremost—a people business!

Now that you know *where* to go, *how* should you proceed?

- *More Is Not Always Better.* John's experience at Microsoft illustrates the importance of building teams that meet specific needs. So focus your efforts by creating a "Top Ten" list of candidates who can introduce you to prospects or provide you with some other competitive advantage. They may be industry pundits or leading thinkers such as scientists or educators. They may run prominent businesses or head up important trade organizations. Carefully consider how *you* can benefit *them* too. Then check the chart above to see where you're most likely to encounter each of them.

- *Be Prepared.* You never know when a networking opportunity will arise, so make sure you always have pertinent information on hand about yourself and your company.

- *Don't Lecture, Listen!* People at networking events want to talk about themselves, and you need to let them!

- *Be Engaged.* Never lead with your "Elevator Pitch." People don't want to be "sold." They want to meet interesting people with balanced lives. Share your personal side. Smile and be enthusiastic. Strive to make a connection, be authentic, and remember to ask more questions than you answer.

- *Give to Get.* Good relationships benefit both parties, so be sure to ask everyone you meet to share his or her goals and objectives.

- *Follow-up.* This is the key to networking success. Send personal notes to your best candidates thanking them for their time. Share a bit of pertinent news about an upcoming industry event or let them know you've made an introduction on their behalf. Most importantly, follow up on your commitments to do something for them!

- ***Never Stop Networking***. As you can see, building your Outside ROPE team is an ongoing process that requires careful planning and dedication. Your network will be critical to your long-term success, so develop it with diligence and care!

In sales, change is a constant. Industry-leading technologies suddenly become obsolete. New competitors enter our markets. We suddenly find ourselves struggling to keep up. At times like these, you'll want to reach out to the industry experts and business leaders on your Outside ROPE team and draw on their wisdom and experience. They will help you adapt to change, regain your momentum, and pursue your vision with fresh motivation and confidence.

Building an Outside ROPE team like this can begin with something as simple as joining a local business or civic organization. Kemper Freeman, CEO of Bellevue, Washington–based Kemper Development Company, has been a member of the Rotary Club for decades. He attends local weekly meetings and also visits clubs whenever he travels domestically or internationally. Today the firm he founded in 1980 is among the most successful real estate development firms in the industry, with a total of four million square feet of Washington State real estate development to its credit, including the Bellevue Collection, comprised of the well-known Bellevue Square, Bellevue Place, and Lincoln Square. According to Freeman, "My entire life, I've lived by the principle that building a community is one of life's greatest rewards. To me, building community means working together, understanding each other, and creating opportunities that are mutually beneficial for everyone."

In recent years, the need for businesses to network has gained such urgency that it has spawned a number of new high-growth businesses. One of them is Eccelerent, a business development company that has retained Sue to give keynote speeches at several of its high-profile company events. As noted on the company's Web site, "Within each local market, we interview and select the right companies to join us in creating a strategic and efficiently managed platform where decision makers can build relationships with other decision makers for the sole purpose of growing their respective companies." Members can use this platform to close deals and build new relationships. For example, an Eccelerent client can use the network to find a partner that is already doing business with a company the member is targeting. The partner can then arrange for the member to meet the prospect at an Eccelerent event. When companies engage with each other and exchange favors in this way, their Outside ROPE teams can become powerful agents of rapid growth.

The Puja Ceremony and the Power of Teams

For the past fifty years, climbers from every corner of the globe have been united by a common goal: to stand atop Mount Everest, the world's highest mountain. These climbers, along with their Sherpa support teams, represent a diverse blend of nationalities, cultures, religions, and philosophies.

On the mountain, however, they must quickly overcome these differences and unite into a smoothly functioning unit, communicating effectively, sharing responsibilities, executing assignments, and taking care of one another. They have no other choice. They can't do it alone.

Collectively these climbing teams must work together to insert more than three hundred ice screws to anchor the three miles of rope needed to safely traverse the icy, dangerous slopes. No team arrives at Base Camp with that much gear. Instead, each team brings a section of what will eventually become a continuous safety-line system.

The Puja Ceremony. *(Sue Ershler)*

After arriving at Everest Base Camp in early April 2001, John, Sue, Phil, and dozens of other climbers finished unloading the tons of climbing gear, food, and supplies they would need during the months of climbing ahead. The most important member of that year's climbing team arrived the following morning—the Lama, or Tibetan "high priest" and teacher of the dharma, the law that Buddhists believe upholds, supports, and maintains the regulatory order of the universe. Without dharma, nothing can stand.

Sherpas will not partner with any team until it has been blessed by a Lama during a sacred Puja Ceremony. And without Sherpa support, a safe and successful climb is nearly impossible.

In preparation for the ceremony, the Sherpas had built the Puja, a stone altar with a niche where a juniper fire would burn whenever a climber was on the upper mountain. Next to it stood an offering of a large container filled with drinks and candy. With the teams gathered before him, the Lama began to chant the Puja prayer requesting permission to climb the mountain and asking for protection and good weather.

Then he blessed everyone in the climbing team, tying a red string around each of their necks to protect them from danger. The Sherpas patted each climber's face with flour, a tradition signifying a life lived to a very old age. Many of the climbers drank Chhaang, a Nepalese/Tibetan alcoholic beverage. Finally the Lama blessed the camp, the climbing equipment, and the colorful prayer flags that the Sherpa had strung from a pole affixed to the altar. Sue also asked the Lama to bless the necklace her parents had given her before she departed for Nepal.

On that day, standing together before the Puja, the disparate groups of climbers joined together to become one unified team. The red strings they wore symbolized their sacred commitment to help each other achieve their shared vision of reaching the summit and then returning safely.

John and Sue would wear their red strings proudly until they finally came apart a year after they returned home.

In this chapter, we discussed the importance of teams in helping you achieve top performer status. Next, we showed you how to build effective teams that generate warm leads and help you secure the internal resources you need to lead a sales campaign to a successful conclusion. Remember:

✓ Don't be a soloist. In the long term, **teams outperform individuals.**

✓ Leverage your Inside Route planning to cross company crevasses and build your **Inside ROPE** team.

✓ Successful **relationships** benefit both parties. So commit yourself to helping everyone on your team achieve their **vision and goals**.

✓ If you want to secure company resources and support, be an evangelist. Make sure to **communicate** effectively and often with key players throughout your organization.

✓ When planning for a meeting, **think like a CEO**. Assemble a team with the right mix of skills. Anticipate questions, defuse conflicts, and orchestrate the proceedings.

✓ **Follow up** after every meeting to ensure that every member of your team fulfills their client commitments.

✓ Build your **Outside ROPE** team by targeting influential industry and business figures and then meeting them where they congregate. Never stop **networking!**

6

EXECUTE THE ROUTE

Mount Kilimanjaro. *(Sue Ershler)*

You will never do anything in this world without courage. It is the greatest quality of the mind next to honor.

—Aristotle

Mount Kilimanjaro is a dormant volcano located in Tanzania. Towering 19,341 feet above sea level, it's not only the highest mountain in Africa but also the highest freestanding mountain in the world.

Iconic Mount Kilimanjaro is often the first hurdle for climbers seeking to fulfill their dream of completing the Seven Summits. Although the mountain is not overly steep or glaciated, its immense height can make it extremely difficult to prepare for, especially for North American climbers like Sue, who must gauge their ability to "go high" by training on smaller mountains.

Almost every climber who attempts to summit Kilimanjaro knows he or she will contend with the headaches, nausea, and shortness of breath that can accompany the milder forms of altitude sickness. Some, despite their best efforts to acclimatize, will see their Kilimanjaro dream shattered by a life-threatening encounter with pulmonary or cerebral edema.

At age thirty-six, Sue had climbed only one mountain— the 14,411-foot Mount Rainier. Now she was about to venture abroad for the first time to test herself on the slopes of Kilimanjaro. She would need to climb nearly 5,000 feet higher than ever before, most of it on a 4,000-vertical-foot nighttime push to reach the summit.

As expected, Sue performed well during the first five days of the climb, arriving at High Camp feeling strong and prepared. She had been close to this altitude before and knew what to expect. That night, she and her team made their bid for the summit.

At high altitudes, dehydration and physical effort can quickly take their toll. Just an hour earlier Sue had felt great. Now, she was exhausted and nauseated. Defeat loomed.

Sue dug down deep, refocusing on her vision and recommitting to her goal. Hours later, she reached the summit and then descended safely. By performing at the high level required to execute her plan, she gained the confidence she needed to continue her quest, and ultimately, to fulfill her dream of conquering the Seven Summits.

Consider how far you've come since chapter 1. We've guided you through the **Project** phase of high achievement as well as through most of the **Prepare** phase. You're well on your way to earning the rewards and recognition that accrue to top performers.

Preparing to Execute the Route

In chapter 7, we'll examine what it takes to **Persevere**; to overcome obstacles and consistently meet and exceed your goals. In this chapter, we'll consider what it takes to "Execute the Route" and perform at the highest levels. This is the phase where the rubber meets the road, where you'll apply your hard-won skills and careful preparation to initiate, manage, and close business.

But first, let's recap what you've learned so far. Start by reviewing the Project and Prepare Checklist chart below. Then spend some quality time with the Project and Prepare worksheets that follow. Write down your goals and confirm that you've taken the necessary preparatory steps to Perform and Persevere. Be sure to update these worksheets during your daily Base Camp sessions to gauge your progress and stay on track!

Project and Prepare Checklist

✓ Project	✓ Prepare
✓ Create Your Vision. "I will be the number one sales representative in my company."	✓ Reflect and Reload. Commit to a continuous process of self-evaluation, goal realignment, and professional development.
✓ Set Specific Goals. Write them down and revisit them often.	✓ Travel the Inside Route. Become an expert on your company, products, and services.

✓ Work Backward. Define all the steps and activities required to achieve your vision.	✓ Travel the Outside Route. Develop the industry expertise and market insights you'll need to serve as your client's trusted guide.
✓ Travel Light. Prioritize, schedule, and track your daily tasks and activities with a time management system.	✓ Cross the Ice Bridge. Help your client succeed by listening to them and then sharing your knowledge and experience. Think like a guide, not a salesperson!
	✓ Identify the New Route. Challenge and reframe the client perceptions you identified during SPIN analysis.
	✓ Present the Confident Route. This is the solution your company is uniquely equipped to provide, one that ensures both you and your client will be successful.
	✓ Cross Company Crevasses to build your Inside ROPE Team. Top performers reach across department lines to recruit talented colleagues, support them in achieving their own goals, and then recognize their contributions to closing business.
	✓ Network to build your Outside ROPE Team. Target and recruit industry experts and business leaders in the settings where they're most likely to congregate. They can play an essential role in helping you find and close business.

Project Worksheet	
Set Your Goal	Top performers fully commit to achieving their goals.
What will you do?	Write down your Summit Goal beginning with the phrase, "I will . . ."
"If you don't know where you're going, you will end up somewhere else."—Yogi Berra	Who will you share your goal with to keep you on track? Where will you post your goal so you see it every day?
	How will you communicate your goal to your team?
	How will you inspire your team to share your goal and help you succeed?
Travel Light	
Prioritize	List three tasks you can eliminate from your current "to do" list:
Use a time management system and schedule your activities.	1. 2. 3.
	List three ways to reduce the time you spend each day on administrative tasks:
	1. 2. 3.
	List three ways to increase your face time with customers:
	1. 2. 3.
	What was the most important thing you did today to make meaningful progress in reaching your goal?

Prepare Worksheet	
Reflect and Reload	
Track your sales performance.	How would you grade your sales achievement: Last week? A ___ B ___ C ___ D ___ F ___ Last month? A ___ B ___ C ___ D ___ F ___ Last quarter? A ___ B ___ C ___ D ___ F ___ Last year? A ___ B ___ C ___ D ___ F ___
Assess your sales skills.	What skills and knowledge do you need to develop to successfully navigate the Inside and Outside Routes?
Commit to ongoing professional development.	Create a plan to strengthen these skills and then track your progress.
Realign your goals!	What changes have you made to your ultimate goal?
Communicate with your team.	How will you measure team success this sales period?
The Inside Route	
Become an expert:	
About your company.	Can you clearly articulate your company's mission, strengths, and core values?
About your products.	Do you fully understand your company's products and technologies?
About your services.	What service and support options does your company offer?

Prepare Worksheet	
The Outside Route	
Create and update Market Plans.	How would you assess your knowledge of the industries and market segments in which you compete? List the markets for which you've developed a Market Plan: 1. 2. 3.
Create and update Account Plans.	Make a list of your top ten to fifteen accounts. Now, list at least three for which you've developed an Account Plan: 1. 2. 3.
Guiding Customers	
Think like a guide, not a salesperson.	Have you committed yourself to helping clients achieve their vision and goals? Have you earned your client's trust by listening? Do you fully understand each client's perceptions about their business needs and solution requirements? Have you challenged these perceptions and guided them to the New Route?
Educate your client.	List three recent examples in which you challenged your client's perceptions and guided them to the New Route: 1. 2. 3.
Propose Confident solutions!	List three ways in which a recent solution you proposed could only be delivered and implemented by your company:

	1.
	2.
	3.
Commit to mutual success.	List three ways in which your Confident solution helped your client succeed:
	1.
	2.
	3.
Networking	
Cross company crevasses.	How many talented employees have you recruited for your Inside ROPE team over the past six months? List the departments and roles for your three newest members. Describe how you recognized their contributions and/or shared your success.
	1.
	2.
	3.
Reach out to your market.	During the past six months, how many networking events have you attended? How many decision makers/industry experts joined your Outside ROPE team? List the three newest members and describe how each relationship is mutually beneficial.
	1.
	2.
	3.

Navigating the Competitive Sales Route

Now that you've reviewed the Project and Prepare checklist and completed the worksheets, it's time to apply your skills and Perform by navigating **The Competitive Sales Route (TCSR)**.

As you can see, **TCSR** consists of seven steps executed in the following four distinct phases.

1. In the **TREK** phase, you'll build your pipeline by finding prospects, setting appointments, and perfecting your pitch.

2. In the **CLIMB** phase, you'll meet with clients, propose solutions, and negotiate pricing and service options.

3. In the **SUMMIT** phase, you'll close the deals you've been nurturing so carefully.

4. In the **RETURN** phase, you'll ensure that your client is successful and recognize everyone on your ROPE teams. This will provide a solid foundation for your ongoing success.

Each of these four phases is detailed further in figure 4.

Now let's explore each phase and its role in helping you Perform at the elite level.

Phase 1: The Trek

In the spring of 2001, John, Sue, and their teammates flew eighty-five miles from Kathmandu, Nepal, to the tiny Sherpa town of Lukla to begin their journey to the top of the world. Their first challenge was to make the forty-mile trek to Base Camp, ascending nine thousand feet as they passed through such Sherpa villages as Namche Bazaar, Tengboche, Pheriche, and Gorak Shep. Only after they completed this two-week trek would the true climb begin.

A trek is a high-altitude hike, devoid of glaciers, crevasses, ice fields, and other technical challenges. The trek brings the climber to the action, so getting there in good form is critical.

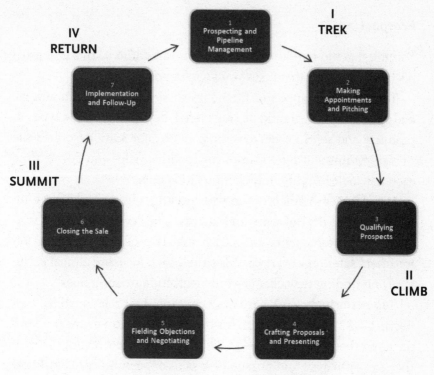

Figure 4: The Four Phases of TCSR

Successful climbers know they must "approach the trek with Intention." They carry sufficient weight to prepare for the physical demands ahead and make sure to acclimatize their bodies gradually to the changing altitude. Most importantly, they begin the mental transition from trekker to climber that prepares them to summit the highest mountains in the world. Sue and John arrived at Base Camp healthy, fit, and prepared for the challenges ahead. Thanks to their yearlong process of projection and preparation, they were ready to execute climbing Everest.

Prospecting

You must get to a mountain before you can climb it. In sales, prospecting is the trek that takes you to an opportunity.

Traditional prospecting methods, such as cold calls, mailings, and special events, should be considered, depending on the types of products and services you're selling. In chapter 3, we described the "Thirty Minutes at Base Camp" process that helps you devote time each day to developing new client relationships.

Don't forget to reach out to your existing clients too! You've invested a great deal of time and energy into developing these relationships. These clients are your *best* source of new business. Yet too often, sales reps overlook this simple fact, focusing almost exclusively on finding new clients while neglecting existing ones.

Top performers work hard to strengthen their relationships, connecting with their clients on an ongoing basis to ensure they understand their emerging needs. They update their Account Plans so they can anticipate and pursue new sales opportunities. They know that maintaining a high level of customer touch is a surefire way to meet and exceed their quota.

In 1996, Sue and her sales team at Verizon found a creative way to leverage her skills as a sales leader and mountain climber to strengthen her firm's relationship with a major client.

> While serving as regional sales manager for major accounts, I was approached by two of my top-performing senior account managers, Pat Sweeney and Kevin Kosche, about arranging a new round of team-building activities with Microsoft, the largest and most significant of our major accounts. Previously we'd organized several reasonably successful outings with our Microsoft counterparts, including a round of paintball competitions. But somehow, shooting at each other with paint guns didn't enhance our relationship as much as we'd hoped. Clearly we needed to try a different kind of

team-building exercise that would unite us in meeting a common goal. Pat and Kevin came up with a great idea. They suggested we invite the Microsoft team to join us in climbing Mount Rainier, with my husband, Phil, serving as our guide.

Before long, we had assembled a team of twelve climbers from Microsoft and twelve more from our Microsoft sales and services team. Our next step was to arrange a meeting in a private room at a local restaurant to brief the teams about the gear they'd be carrying on the mountain and how they should prepare physically for the rigors of the climb. There was very little socializing or chitchat. Everyone left promptly when the briefing ended. It was not the most auspicious start for a team-building exercise. Still, we all hoped for the best.

Several weeks later, the twenty-four of us were crammed together in a mountain hut perched at 10,000 feet, preparing

Team building with Microsoft. *(Phil Ershler)*

ourselves for our midnight push to Rainier's summit at 14,410 feet. The climb that followed was tough and challenging. But after several hours, we made it to the summit. As we celebrated together, we knew that our relationship had reached a new level of mutual trust and respect.

This was confirmed a week later, when we met in the same private room in the same restaurant, this time to celebrate our success. The atmosphere was completely different. Everyone was talking, laughing, and sharing photos. No one was in a hurry to leave. We had forged a meaningful bond, one that would grow and strengthen for years to come.

The digital age has created exciting new ways to reach out to prospects. A wealth of information about companies and decision makers can be accessed instantly via Internet searches and social media sites such as LinkedIn and Facebook. Customer Relationship Management ("CRM") systems can be deployed to organize, analyze, manage, and act on this information easily and efficiently.

These innovations and those yet to come are fundamentally changing the buyer/seller relationship. Today, prospects can independently perform in-depth research about virtually every kind of product or service. They can learn about the latest technologies and the companies that are most likely to compete for their business. They can compare and contrast solutions and join online forums and user groups to read unbiased critiques from your existing clients.

As a result, the power dynamic has changed, with buyers increasingly taking charge by defining their solution requirements and sellers forced to compete based on price and service options alone. In chapter 4, we described how to overcome these challenges by winning client trust and then guiding them to the New Route.

In response, sellers are deploying Web sites that invite potential clients to engage in an ongoing dialogue while drawing them closer by parceling out useful information. They may monitor online forums to offer information and respond to postings while carefully avoiding any appearance of overt selling. Skillfully done, this can be a productive way to attract prospects.

Whatever methods you choose, prospecting is the inevitable first step in the selling process. It's essential but never easy—just like the forty-mile trek to Everest Base Camp!

Cold Calling Is Cold

Climbers go to great lengths to stay warm. As the body cools, energy stores are depleted much more quickly and there is a real danger of hypothermia and death.

In sales, cold calling won't kill you, but it can sometimes feel that way. More importantly, it's an extremely inefficient approach to prospecting. Just as a warm climber can go higher, a warm introduction to a new prospect offers much better odds for landing a sale.

The Outside ROPE team you began assembling in chapter 5 will begin to pay dividends when people within your business community know what you do and where you work. Association leads to referrals. *"You should meet my friend Karyn. She works for a search engine optimization company that could really drive traffic to your Web site."*

When you carefully cultivate your Outside ROPE team, you gain a warm entrée to prospects who have already learned about you from someone they trust, saving you time and focusing your efforts where they can be most beneficial for you and your company.

For some companies, the commitment to build strong Outside ROPE teams is ingrained into the company culture and expands beyond the sales sphere to encompass a broad array of initiatives in community relations and corporate philanthropy.

One such company is Windermere Real Estate, a preeminent residential real estate firm with offices in Alaska, Hawaii, and nine western states. Windermere has more than five hundred franchise locations and continues to thrive while many industry peers have struggled. The company attributes its success to its investments in networking and its commitment to improving the communities in which it conducts business.

The company pursues these goals operationally at each local office by deploying employees—known internally as Go Givers—who are charged with establishing community partnerships and with sharing the firm's technology and best practices expertise at industry events and conferences. These efforts have proven to be successful in attracting new franchisees to join the Windermere family. Go Givers also focus on reaching out to franchise owners across the Windemere network to build an extended Outside ROPE team that can share expertise and collaborate on projects.

Additionally Windermere donates a portion of its revenue to support low-income and homeless families through its Windermere Foundation. The company also encourages franchise owners to build relationships with local nonprofit organizations and to participate actively in community events.

Thanks to this strategic and comprehensive approach to Outside ROPE team building, Windermere's business has grown exponentially, a classic "doing well by doing good" scenario that benefits its franchises, its communities, and the industry as a whole.

Targeting Accounts

Your Market and Account plans armed you with a wealth of new insights about the companies in each of the regions and industry segments you sell into. Now you can utilize this information while prospecting to focus on the best candidates. Here's an example of the criteria you might use to choose your targets.

- *Marketing leads*: The marketing department is responsible for setting strategy, defining products, and generating leads and market awareness to assist the sales department in closing business.

Ideally, both departments report to the same individual to ensure they work together in lockstep. The marketing department can provide you with invaluable strategic guidance in selecting your targets and penetrating accounts. Be willing to cross company crevasses and recruit talented marketing professionals to join your Inside ROPE team.

- *Your competitor's clients*: These companies have already demonstrated their appreciation for products and services like yours by investing time, money, and resources in acquiring them. However, they may not have fully realized the benefits they expected, especially if their salesperson overpromised or if the supplier failed some aspect of implementation. Dislodging an incumbent can be difficult, so this sales cycle may take longer. But it's well worth the effort. Be sure to target the companies these prospects compete against too. You may discover they are actively seeking solutions like yours to maintain their competitive edge.

- *Companies with aging, inefficient, or obsolete products:* Ask your Outside ROPE team to help you flag companies that are dissatisfied and ready to consider replacing, upgrading, or augmenting products and services like those offered by your company.

- *Companies with budgets and time frames that meet your quota goals and objectives*: This is one of the keystones of the qualification process, which we'll examine shortly. Suffice it to say that an unhappy company doesn't become a prospect until they've set aside a budget and assigned a buying team. Too often, sales people devote considerable time and energy to these "opportunities" only to see them fail at the critical pricing and negotiation phase. Be sure to focus your efforts on prospects that are ready and able to buy.

- *Companies in vertical markets*: You may have been assigned to a vertical market or selected one that aligns with your experience and expertise. Either way, vertical selling affords an efficient and productive approach to prospecting. With every sale, you'll gain new industry insights, master new terminology, and learn to craft replicable solutions that are perfectly tailored to companies in that sector. You'll also forge new relationships to expand your Outside ROPE Team, leading to new sector-specific referrals that can prove invaluable in the future.

- **Companies that are a perfect fit for the Confident Route**: Every now and then, you may encounter a prospect with solution requirements that seem custom-made to your products and services. If your company is uniquely qualified to win, go for it!

Setting Up Appointments—The First Sale

Once you find a prospect, your next challenge is to "sell" them on meeting with you. It's unlikely you'll snag the decision maker on your first call. At this stage, your goal is to secure a meeting with anyone who has a vested interest in the kinds of products and services you offer. This could be anyone—the IT technician, a human resources representative, or even a part-time administrator. Contacts like these may lack the authority to approve a sale, but they will often participate on the buying team as "influencers."

Be respectful and courteous to everyone who is willing to meet with you. You only have one chance to make a first impression, so be sure to prepare and practice your "pitch."

The pitch is much more than a generic presentation or elevator speech. It sets the tone for the entire sales process. Although your pitch may vary, depending on the audience and situation, it should always include such key elements as your company's mission and core strengths. Carefully consider whom you will be speaking with, what their concerns are, and the nature of their business. Then craft your message accordingly.

During your first meeting, focus on achieving three simple goals:

1. *Introduce yourself and your company.* Thanks to your Inside Route preparation, you've become an articulate and convincing spokesperson. Describe your company's mission, markets, core values, and reputation. Highlight its three greatest strengths. Most importantly, be sure to connect on a personal level. It's not yet time to sell anything!

2. *Prequalify your prospect to determine if they represent a real sales opportunity.* You may feel awkward asking probing questions and want to avoid any chance of hearing the dreaded word *no*. But it's far better to cut your losses now, before you devote valuable time and energy to an opportunity that may never have truly existed.
   - If the meeting came through a referral, try an approach like, "Our mutual friend mentioned that your company is considering a new wireless networking solution. Can you tell me more about that?"
   - If the meeting is the result of a cold call, you might say something like, "As you know, I'm a sales representative for Dell. Is your company planning to make any workstation changes this year?"

3. *Make a friend and determine next steps.* Don't be discouraged if the prospect expresses little or no interest in what you have to offer. You've scored a valuable opportunity to *add* a new member to your Outside ROPE team. As you would in any networking setting, ask your new friend how you can help him or her achieve their goals and then follow through on your commitments. You can be sure you'll hear from them when their situation changes and they're ready to buy. If they've already reached the point of considering a purchase, conclude the meeting by determining next steps and then add the company to your prospect list. You've got a live one!

Measuring the Mountain—Manage Your Pipeline

On the mountain, we know how many feet we have to climb each day to reach the summit. In sales, we track our progress in meeting our quota goal through pipeline management.

Your pipeline is a critically important tool in your sales arsenal. It should provide an accurate snapshot of where you stand with all of your prospects, allowing you to adjust and correct your daily activities before you drift off course and miss your numbers.

Management will hold you accountable for your pipeline. So be honest and keep it real. If you lose a deal, remove it from your pipeline. If a prospect stops responding, make a final effort to reach out to them and then move them to a separate list. Check in with them from time to time to see if they're ready to begin the buying process.

Assign a status to each of your active prospects and then update this as the sales process unfolds. Each status corresponds to a sales stage and a "likely to close" percentage and time frame. This data will provide the basis for your sales forecasts.

The information used to define these stages will vary from company to company and reflect management's experience with sales in previous years. If your company uses an enterprise-wide sales force automation program like salesforce.com, the stages will already have been defined for you and incorporated into the system. In that case, simply apply the relevant milestone to each opportunity as it progresses through your pipeline. Be sure to review and update this status every day during your Thirty-Minute Base Camp sessions.

Let's take a look at a sample pipeline management approach that breaks the sales tracking process into five distinct stages.

1. You've conducted an initial meeting and jointly agreed on a series of next steps.

2. The prospect has assigned a budget to purchase the kinds of product or service you sell and selected your company to be

among those competing for their business. The prospect has now been prequalified and become a legitimate opportunity.

3. You've submitted a proposal and know the time frame in which they plan to make the purchase decision. This projected close date will be used to update your forecast and track your progress against your weekly, monthly, quarterly, and annual sales quotas.

4. Your company has been selected as a finalist in the competition.

5. Your company has won, contingent on final negotiations about pricing, service levels, and other relevant terms and conditions.

Here's how these stages might be reflected in a typical pipeline tracking report.

Company	Contact	E-mail	Phone	Last Mtg.	Situation: Proposed	Next Steps	Status
Microsoft	***	***	***	7/15/13	New prospect. Proposed 22 J5 workstations.	Meet with decision maker	1
Starbucks	***	***	***	8/1/13	Selling into new division. Proposed 105 K7 workstations.	Presenting to division head 8/5.	2
Boeing	***	***	***	7/22/13	Customer for 4 years. Add-on order for 175 C9 tablets.	Letter of Agreement signed. Final pricing mtg. 8/6.	5
FedEx	***	***	***	7/18/13	Competing for the first time. One of 2 finalists. Proposed 330 C9 tablets.	We are a finalist. Second presentation 8/10.	4
Safeco	***	***	***	8/2/13	Competing for the first time. Proposed 10 J5 workstations. Concerned with lack of communication.	Presented first proposal on 8/2. No response.	2/3

Managing your pipeline not only is important to you and your manager, but also plays a critical role in helping executive management run the business. Your pipeline will be consolidated with those of your colleagues to create detailed, quarter-by-quarter revenue forecasts that will help drive critical corporate decisions about manufacturing, staffing levels, acquisitions, expansion into new markets, and much more. If your company is public, errors in forecasting can lead to earnings calls where the reported results fall short of analyst expectations, causing the stock price to tumble and, potentially, forcing major changes to company strategy.

Without ongoing prospecting, your pipeline will quickly evaporate and you will have no one to sell to—nowhere to *climb*! So top performers approach the sales trek with great seriousness and treat prospecting as a full-time job.

During his first year in sales, John left his office at Xerox early every morning to search for new customers. Most of the prospects he met denied his meeting requests. He found this process to be extremely tiring and tiresome.

Noticing his frustration, John's regional sales manager, Jay Tyler, reminded him that he could control only two things: his attitude and the activities he performed to achieve his sales goals. John was already doing a terrific job with cold calling, networking, targeting accounts, and seeking referrals. So Jay suggested that John change his attitude toward prospecting. Rather than seeing it as a chore, he could view it as an opportunity to make a new friend every day. This attitude shift yielded huge dividends. Suddenly, prospecting was fun! John rapidly expanded his pipeline and went on to become the top performer in his sales group that year.

Case Study and Quiz

Let's apply the prospecting and pipeline management concepts we've been discussing to a real-world—albeit entirely fictional— sales scenario.

Brookline Systems sales representatives Andy and Brooke sell computer systems. Each system is counted as a "unit," although the revenue per unit may vary. To meet their monthly quotas, each rep must sell at least five units that generate $100,000 or more in revenues.

On January 15, their sales manager summoned both of them to a pipeline meeting to review the status of their accounts and to assess their progress in reaching their monthly goal. In the charts below, we show each rep's numbers and where they actually finished the month. Study the information below.

Question: Who is in trouble with their sales manager—Andy or Brooke?

Andy: Pipeline Status 1/15/14				Andy: Actual Sales Results 1/31/14		
Account	Units	Revenue	Status	Account	Units	Revenue
A	2	$25,000	5	A	1	$5,000
B	1	$20,000	4	C	5	$90,000
C	3	$40,000	1	D	0	Lost
D	1	$25,000	5	E	4	$50,000
Total	7	$110,000			10	$145,000
Brooke: Pipeline Status 1/15/14				Brooke: Actual Sales Results 1/31/14		
Account	Units	Revenue	Status	Account	Units	Revenue
F	2	$35,000	5	F	2	$35,000
G	1	$25,000	5	G	1	$25,000
H	2	$20,000	1			
I	1	$10,000	2			
Total	6	$90,000			3	$60,000

Answer: Andy had a very difficult meeting with his sales manager while Brooke was commended, but encouraged to do *more*!

How can that be, when Andy blew away both his unit quota *and* his revenue quota while Brooke came up short on both?

Looking at these charts, we can conclude that Andy is a long way from mastering the skills needed to successfully traverse the TCSR. Accounts A and D were tagged with status 5—so both of them should have closed. Instead, Andy lost Account D and sold far less than he expected to Account A. He also failed to close *any* business with Account B, which he had tagged with a status of 4. Worst of all, his biggest sale, Account E, wasn't even being tracked as a likely win on his pipeline report from just two weeks before. Andy was lucky to have sold anything!

In contrast, Brooke's pipeline report is right on the money. Both her 5's closed, and she has three units in the pipeline. She clearly knows what she's doing but needs to increase her activity level and grow her prospect list. Brooke has mastered the TCSR process and is well on her way to becoming a top performer.

Phase 2: The Climb

In chapters 3 and 4, you learned how to identify and target your top-tier customers and help guide them to success. In this section, we'll consider the best ways to document and deliver your New Route recommendations.

Qualifying Your Prospect

You've prequalified your prospect by confirming they're in the market for your product or service. They've set a time frame for making the purchasing decision. However, these plans and timelines can always change, so you must continue qualifying until the deal closes. Here are some key factors that can influence your prospect's decision-making process and derail a deal.

- **Competition**. Your competitors are just as determined as you are to close business. At every point in the sales process, ask your prospect if you're fulfilling their expectations and if anything has changed that would affect your working relationship.

- **Budget**. No budget is set in stone. Your prospect may decide to cut spending after a bad quarter. New decision makers may enter the scene with their own sets of priorities and requirements. When that happens, move swiftly to meet with them to introduce yourself and recap your activities up to that point. Be sensitive to their budget concerns. This doesn't mean lowering your price. But you may have to modify the scope or timing of your proposed solution to reflect what they can now afford.

- **Priorities**. The energy and enthusiasm you bring to a meeting may be so contagious that your prospect seems to be rocketing toward a favorable decision. But this may not actually be the case. Does your solution address at least one of their most pressing priorities? Or is it simply a "nice to have" that they're considering because of your outstanding people skills?

- **Remember the vitamins versus aspirin test**. If you wake up with excruciating tooth pain, you may very well decide to get out of bed and drive to the store to buy aspirin. Few of us would behave the same way if we ran out of vitamins. Aspirin decisions take priority over vitamin decisions. It's your job to make sure your prospect fully appreciates the importance of the problems your solution addresses and considers solving them to be a high priority. In today's business world, priorities can change on a dime. So if your solution is no longer a high priority, change your pipeline status and forecast to reflect this.

Proposing a Solution

The proposal is the culmination of your information gathering, applied research, and creative solution design. It documents your New Route recommendations and incorporates your **Situation, Problem, Implication**, and **Needs** analysis.

Although it may contain standard product descriptions and terminology, your proposal should be as specific and customized to your prospect as possible. If it's not, you may be perceived as pushing a generic "one size fits all" solution and lose your prospect's trust. Timing is critical too. The proposal should be submitted only after you have challenged your prospect's assumptions and established your New and Confident routes. If you move to the proposal stage too soon, you may find yourself demoted from the status of guide to that of mere salesperson.

The proposal shouldn't contain any surprises. It should accurately reflect the sales process and the decisions that led to your specific recommendations. It should also address pricing, implementation schedules, and any other pertinent information.

You should assume that your proposal will be circulated to every member of the purchasing team, even those you were unable to meet. Your advocates within the company will do their best to convey the strengths of your solution to these unseen influencers and decision makers. But they will never do this as effectively and persuasively as you would. So make sure that your proposal is complete, clearly written, cleanly formatted, and professional in every respect. Don't forget to spell-check!

Presenting Your Solution

Good news! Your prospect has invited you to present your proposal. This is *not* an opportunity to walk them laboriously through every page and recite every word of your carefully crafted prose. Most likely, they've already read your proposal. So prepare a presentation that brings your proposal to life and communicates your key points concisely and gracefully.

- Introduce yourself and any team members you've brought along with you.

- Briefly summarize what you've learned about their company and why you're excited by this opportunity to work together.

- Review the scope and importance of the business issues you've identified and the resulting challenges and opportunities your solution will address. Be sure to recognize and thank everyone on their team for sharing their time and expertise with you.

- Provide a concise description of your proposed solution and its benefits, along with the associated pricing and implementation details.

- Set aside sufficient time for a question-and-answer session.

Handling Objections

Although we're introducing this topic in the context of presenting a proposal, you can expect to encounter objections at every point in the sales process. You may feel that they're an indication that you're losing a sale, but this is not necessarily the case. Objections can often be extremely useful. They can help you shape and fine-tune your solution, so embrace them!

Top performers never stop listening to their customers and prospects. If one of your contacts voices an objection, listen carefully to make sure you fully understand their concerns. Don't get defensive.

Demonstrate that you understand by repeating their objection in your own words and asking them if you heard it correctly. This gives them an opportunity to clarify their position and provide additional details.

Many objections are the result of a miscommunication that can quickly be corrected. Others may expose shortcomings in your company or proposed solutions. It's essential that you acknowledge these concerns and find ways to mitigate them. If you're up-front and honest, you'll enhance your credibility and disarm your critics.

Let's consider one of the most common objections we encounter as salespeople: pricing. If your solution costs more than the competition, this must be explained and justified. Is your prospect making an "apples to apples" comparison? If your solution is more expensive because it includes a richer set of services and functionality, be sure to point this out. Of course, you must be sure that the enhancements you've included are necessary to meet the client's goals. All too often, deals are lost when a salesperson proposes a solution filled with unnecessary bells and whistles that price them out of the competition.

If you're confident that your solution delivers the optimal combination of price and value, try justifying the higher price by focusing on:

- The superior quality of your products, services, and company.

- Your firm's proven track record in delivering solutions like these on time and on budget.

- The total lifetime costs, including maintenance and upgrades.

- The most dangerous kind of objection is the "nonobjection objection." In this case, the prospect isn't being completely candid with you. They may like you personally and want to avoid offending you or hurting your feelings. So they offer a vague objection as a ploy, hoping you can't or won't respond favorably. This strategy gives them a seemingly valid excuse to end the meeting and terminate the sales process.

You can test for a "nonobjection objection" by reframing it as a hypothetical situation. If the objection is to your delivery date, for example, you might ask the prospect, "If we can meet your new time frame, can we move forward?" If they say "Yes, we can," then the objection was a real one and you can revisit the delivery schedule with your team. If the prospect says, "I'm not sure," then you may have a "nonobjection objection" on your hands. Or the prospect may be expressing a genuine objection that masks several others. In this case, keep probing until you've uncovered and addressed all of their objections, one after the next!

Negotiating the Sale

You've presented your proposal and updated it to reflect your prospect's feedback. Now it's time to begin the negotiation process, "giving and getting" as you confirm the final details within the constraints placed by your company on pricing, service commitments, etc. Never overcommit or promise anything your company can't deliver. Your long-term success is contingent on your company's ability to deliver on time and on budget. Always adhere to the Confident Route.

If you run into a roadblock and need executive support, ask for it. Don't overstep your authority or try to function as a lone wolf. As we noted in chapter 5, **teams outperform individuals**.

Phase 3: Reaching the Summit and Closing the Sale

"Closing" is one of the most misunderstood terms in the sales lexicon. It's true, of course, that every sales process must come to an end. But closing is not something that can be forced by bending the client to your will. Most often, closing is the natural culmination of a well-executed sales campaign, with the signed contract the inevitable and final "to do" item.

There's a catch, however. Salespeople don't always recognize when a deal has been won. They may be concerned about offending a prospect by asking for the order. Or they may be unwilling to risk learning that their hard-fought campaign has been lost to a competitor. So they keep pontificating about the benefits of their products or scheduling additional meetings to refine their proposals. They continue selling way past the point where it's necessary or desirable.

Ask yourself, and then your customer, if there's anything else that needs to be accomplished before the contract is signed. You may be surprised to discover that the sales process is over. If you've followed through on each of the steps we outlined above, The Competitive Sales Route will take you to the summit of sales success faster than you might have ever imagined.

Phase 4: The Return

If we are climbing a mountain, then the summit is merely the halfway point in our journey. If we stop there, we will certainly die. A climb is only considered successful if we return safely after reaching the summit. John recalls a moment on the mountain that illustrated this point all too clearly.

> *I had finally reached the summit of Everest. It had taken me more than twelve hours to climb through wicked storms and thin air from Camp IV at 26,000 feet to the summit at 29,035 feet. As I prepared to descend, my climbing partner and their two Sherpas rappelled ahead of me over the daunting Hillary Step. Soon they were out of sight as they navigated down the icy trail.*
>
> *Now, alone and exhausted, I had little energy left to return*

to Camp IV. With my supplies frozen, I hadn't had any food or water for more than fifteen hours. I was ready to stop and I knew what that meant. If I died on the summit, I would void the success that the entire team had worked so hard to achieve over the past few months. I didn't want that.

It was then I remembered that our lead Sherpa had placed a stainless steel thermos full of hot tea in my backpack the night before we started our summit climb. If I wasn't hallucinating, the tea should still be there, providing exactly the jolt of energy I would need to make it back safely.

Newly motivated, I began to climb down faster than before, looking for a safe place to stop and look for my precious thermos. Propelled by the hope of hot tea, I caught up with Greg. We stopped together while I searched my pack. The tea was there! The four of us drank our share and returned safely to High Camp.

Owning the Customer Experience

As a salesperson, you're measured by and held accountable for the quantity and quality of the business you generate. You're not expected to provide the specialized knowledge and expertise required for delivery, implementation, and support. However, this doesn't mean that your job is done once the deal closes. It's your responsibility to "own the customer experience."

If you suddenly disappear from the scene, your customer may feel abandoned and neglected. In extreme cases, they may experience buyer's remorse and try to terminate the deal you've so carefully orchestrated.

Check in with your contacts frequently to ensure they're receiving everything they contracted for. Make sure they're fully satisfied with your company's service and support. As a guide, it's your job to advocate on their behalf if a serious problem arises that isn't being addressed internally. You should also be prepared to intercede if your team encounters a roadblock that requires delicate client hand-holding.

Many sales have been won and lost because the salesperson left the scene prematurely. Conversely, when a salesperson is on hand to listen to the customer, he or she may be able to generate significant follow-on business by proposing lucrative enhancements or expanding the scope of the solution to additional departments or business units. As we emphasized earlier, top performers always maintain a high level of customer touch.

In 1997, Sue's team at Verizon closed one of the biggest deals in the company's history when they won a contract with Microsoft to implement what would prove to be one of the world's largest networks based on Asynchronous Transfer Mode (ATM) technology. At the time, ATM represented a networking breakthrough, enabling companies to consolidate voice, data, and video traffic over a single integrated high-speed network. By eliminating the need for separate voice and data networks, companies like Microsoft could significantly reduce their network equipment and management costs.

Verizon was committed to the new technology. So Sue's team, led by major account managers, Pat and Kevin, spent months on the Inside Route, poring over the details and learning how to effectively position Verizon's ATM product and service offerings. In the campaign that followed, they drew on all of their skills and experiences to Execute the Route. In Sue's words:

> Looking back, I can see how our team applied all of the strategies we've been describing in this book to win the deal.
>
> - **We projected our Vision**. Everyone on our Microsoft sales and services team had a single focus: to develop what Microsoft would recognize as the very best solution to their networking needs,

one that delivered an unbeatable value proposition. We committed ourselves to top performance, devoting many hours to every aspect of our networking proposal.

- **We Reflected and Reloaded**. The previous year, Microsoft had hired a new COO, who subjected all company expenditures to a new and even stricter level of scrutiny. With dismay, Pat and Kevin saw their sales revenues plummet from 200 percent of their quota in Q1 to less than 60 percent by Q4. They responded by putting together an aggressive Reflect and Reload plan that would lead to one of the biggest wins of their careers.

- **We Traveled Light**. Recognizing the strategic importance of this sale, Verizon allowed all seventeen members of our on-site services team to focus exclusively on Microsoft throughout the sales campaign.

- **We crossed company crevasses**. A deal of this scope requires company-wide collaboration. Fortunately, we had established a strong Inside ROPE team that encompassed sales, operations, product management, and finance, among others. We had also earned the respect and cooperation of executive management.

- **We built a solid Outside ROPE team**. Our Rainier expedition was part of a larger, long-term effort to build strong relationships with our Microsoft counterparts, one that stood us in good stead during this sales campaign. We also knew that the solution we were proposing would integrate systems from several different network equipment manufacturers. So we built strong relationships with each of them to ensure we could work together seamlessly and present a united face to the client.

- **We traversed the Outside Route**. Our sales and engineering teams fully understood the business challenges Microsoft's new network was designed to address and developed an Account Plan and Confident Route proposal that would guide the company through implementation and deployment, while paving the way for future upgrades and enhancements.

We were all exhilarated when the months of intense effort the team invested paid off with the news that we had won the deal. After a short celebration, we got back to work, refining our implementation plan, and then doing everything necessary, on-site and off, to deliver exemplary service.

Team Recognition

Your Inside ROPE team has helped you win the deal. Now it's time to share your success by thanking every member of your team.

Do this publicly. Send an e-mail to their managers describing the critical role they played in winning the business or meeting a particularly difficult customer requirement. During the next company meeting, formally recognize each of them for their efforts.

Be sure to acknowledge your Outside ROPE team as well. Then demonstrate your appreciation by fulfilling all of your commitments to help them achieve their goals.

Your Inside and Outside ROPE team members are an indispensable resource: a rich source of support, expertise, and referrals. Make sure they feel valued and appreciated. If you share your success, you will earn their loyalty and respect. They will be eager to join you on your next successful journey across The Competitive Sales Route.

In this chapter, we showed you how to achieve peak performance by Executing the Route. We started by reviewing the Project and Prepare prerequisites to Performance that we addressed in previous chapters. Then we examined the TREK, CLIMB, SUMMIT, and RETURN phases of The Competitive Sales Route. Remember:

Celebrating our team. *(Charlie Peck)*

✓ You must **Project** and **Prepare** before you can **Perform** and **Persevere**.

✓ Complete your **Project** and **Prepare** worksheets at the beginning of every sales cycle and refer to them each morning during your Thirty-Minute Base Camp session.

✓ The Competitive Sales Route is a circular journey that begins and ends with **prospecting**. Consider this one of your top priorities as you create your daily "to do" lists.

✓ **Educate** yourself about potential clients, using both traditional and online methods.

✓ Warm up your cold calls by leveraging your Outside ROPE team and by maintaining **high touch** with your existing clients. Remember that they are your best source of new business.

✓ Be honest and realistic in managing your **sales pipeline**. Top performers **Measure the Mountain** to accurately track their progress.

✓ Don't submit your **proposal** too early. Make sure it's professional and strong enough to stand on its own.

✓ Don't oversell! **Closing** is the natural culmination of a well-executed sales campaign. When it's time, ask for the order!

✓ **Own the customer experience** by staying in close contact with your client after the sales process ends. This is the best way to preserve the trust you've earned as their guide and to create new opportunities for follow-on business.

PART III

PERSEVERE

Hillary Step, Mount Everest. *(John Waechter)*

7

STAND ON TOP

PERSEVERE: All great achievements are realized by committing to a goal and then working relentlessly to attain it—against all odds!

Nothing in this world can take the place of persistence. Talent will not; nothing is more common than unsuccessful people with talent. Genius will not; unrewarded genius is almost a proverb. . . . Persistence and determination alone are omnipotent. The slogan "press on" has solved and always will solve the problems of the human race.

—Calvin Coolidge

At the beginning of chapter 1, John and Sue were battling treacherous weather and their own exhaustion to reach the summit of Mount Everest. Now, as we near the end of our journey together, they have reached the grueling last leg of their climb: the ascent from Camp IV (at 26,000 ft.) to the summit (at 29,035 ft.).

May 25, 2001. Despite the worsening weather, the climbing team resolved to extend their expedition by one day to rest and prepare for their summit bid. While this decision was a sound one, it meant that their window of relatively good weather was one day closer to closing. As they set off from High Camp at 10:00 p.m., destructive monsoon winds were approaching. Had they waited too long?

Accompanied by their five Sherpa helpers, Phil, Sue, John, and their friends Charlie Peck and Greg Wilson trudged up the mountain, where the screaming winds and driving snow created near whiteout conditions. Only a few hours into the climb, Charlie was forced by a long-standing pulmonary condition to turn back. Then, a few hours later, Sue and Phil had to turn back because a faulty oxygen mask had caused Phil's eyes to freeze over. The summit team of ten had now shrunk to just four: John, Greg, and their Sherpa companions.

John and Greg found the prospect of proceeding into a difficult storm without their full team both daunting and difficult. But they were determined to carry on. Around 2:00 a.m., they resumed the treacherous climb from the Balcony into the gathering storm, resolving to stop every thirty minutes to reassess whether or not to continue.

John struggled through the thinning air. As he approached 28,000 feet, he realized that he could no longer feel his hands or his feet. His frozen fingers seemed to grip his ice ax through memory rather than actual sensation.

Finally, the sun started to rise above the distant horizon. Usually, climbers welcome the arrival of the sun after laboring for hours in the darkness, with only the glow of their headlamps to guide them. But at this altitude, the daylight revealed a terrain that was stark and terrifying. Looking around, John felt as if he had been dropped from a jetliner and left to cling precariously to the mountain's edge. He had to take several deep breaths to ward off the spiraling sensation of vertigo that began to overtake him. A few moments later, he was able to stabilize himself and continued up the mountain.

After nine hours of climbing, John and Greg reached the South Summit at 28,700 feet. Their food and water had long since frozen and their climb was about to get even more perilous. Now, with their energy reserves flagging, they would have to ascend the Hillary Step—a nearly vertical, fifty-foot narrow chute named after Sir Edmund Hillary, who, together with legendary Nepalese Sherpa Tenzing Norgay, became the *first climbers to be confirmed as having reached the summit of Everest.*

John and Greg descended down the steep backside of the South Summit and around a knife ridge to the base of the Step. Another hour passed before they reached the top of the chute and embarked on their final march to the summit. At close to 29,000 feet, the air was so thin they had to take six deep breaths before every step. But their goal was now in sight, so they kept moving.

Finally, twelve hours after leaving Camp IV, exhausted but exhilarated, John, Greg, and their two Sherpa teammates stood atop Mount Everest, gazing in wonder at the magnificent view laid out before them. John and Greg had shared similar triumphs before. But this one was different. Although he felt a quiet contentment about reaching the summit, John was not yet ready to celebrate. He knew they had achieved only half their goal. True success wouldn't be theirs until they had descended the mountain and arrived back safely.

The fierce storm they had climbed through hours before was still raging below. Tired, thirsty, hungry, and very low on energy, the four climbers huddled together to plan their descent. Then, moving as quickly as they could, they began the difficult journey down the icy mountain, bracing themselves for the storm awaiting them on their way back to High Camp.

As we begin this chapter, we're coming to the end of *our* journey together. Take a moment now to consider how far you've come.

- You've learned how to Project your vision of personal and professional achievement.

- You've learned how to Prepare yourself by traversing the Inside and Outside Routes to become a guide worthy of earning your client's trust and sharing in their success.

- You've learned how to expand your reach and resources by building and leading your Inside and Outside ROPE teams.

- You've learned how to Perform at an elite level by navigating successfully through the four phases of The Competitive Sales Route.

We've armed you with the knowledge and skills you need to excel. But these are no guarantees of success. If you want to become a top performer, you must be diligent and disciplined in applying the lessons you've learned in previous chapters. You must put our les-sons into practice every day, no matter what obstacles you encounter along the way. You must learn to **persevere**; to exceed your perceived limits and achieve more than you ever thought possible.

Why is it important to persevere? Working hard is, well, *hard*! Committing to work hard *all* of the time is an even more daunting proposition. Making calls and hearing no can take the wind out of anyone's sails. Let's face it. Getting beat hurts. The grind is often painful. Quitting is always an option.

Perseverance is the singular quality that Everest summiteers and top sales performers have in common. They both recognize that pain is temporary. They persevere through thick and thin because they have an inner beacon of confidence to draw upon when the going gets tough. They also choose their teams with care. As Sue's husband, Phil, often said, "Surround yourself with people who won't let you quit."

Perseverance is like a muscle that becomes stronger with exercise and practice. It's a habit that enables you to approach every personal or professional challenge with focus and determination. We believe that perseverance is the key to a successful and rewarding life.

In this final chapter, we'll consider how top performers learn to persevere on their journey to peak achievement and how you can find the strength and motivation to follow their example.

Why Persevere?

John D. Rockefeller once said, "I do not think there is any other quality so essential to success of any kind as the quality of perseverance. It overcomes almost everything, even nature." Throughout history, great leaders have emphasized the role that perseverance played in their lives and inspired others to do the same. Consider these four examples:

- In the dark days of 1941, Winston Churchill returned to his alma mater, the Harrow School, where he gave a commencement address urging students to "never give in. Never give in. Never, never, never, never—in nothing, great or small, large or petty—never give in, except to convictions of honor and good sense."

- During his 1993 ESPY Awards speech, mere weeks before his untimely death, legendary North Carolina State basketball coach Jim Valvano announced the formation of his Jimmy V cancer research foundation. The motto he chose was emblematic of the perseverance he had demonstrated throughout his coaching career: "Don't give up. . . . Don't ever give up!"

- Although he is now recognized as a brilliant showman and movie mogul, success didn't come easily or quickly to Walt Disney. It took him decades to secure the film rights to *Mary Poppins* from author P. L. Travers, who was convinced that no movie could ever do justice to her literary creation. During the two years of production, they continued to spar over the script, the score, the animation, and much more. In the end, the film would become one of Disney's greatest triumphs, earning thirteen Academy Award nominations and winning five awards.

- J. K. Rowling spent seven years writing her first Harry Potter novel. During this period, she was, in her words, "jobless, a lone parent, and as poor as it is possible to be in modern Britain, without being homeless." Her completed manuscript was rejected by twelve publishing houses before finally finding a home at Bloomsbury Publishing. Today, Rowling has won a worldwide audience for her books and film adaptations and—according to *Forbes*—had a net worth of approximately $1 billion in 2012.

Why are leaders like these driven to succeed while others are satisfied with the status quo? Is perseverance an innate capability possessed only by the fortunate few?

Like any human trait, the capacity to persevere varies from person to person. However, these intrinsic differences don't explain why some people become top performers and others don't. We believe that anyone can accomplish great feats if they summon the will required to overcome seemingly insurmountable obstacles.

Successful individuals know how to motivate themselves to achieve peak performance on an ongoing basis. They know what internal levers to pull when their engines of determination start to flag. You too can learn how to tap these inner reserves through insight and practice.

Start with a frank self-assessment. What drives you? Is it money, recognition, or advancement? Top performers reap all of these rewards and more. Consider the "Insight Route" worksheet below and rank your "drivers" from one (least important) to ten (most important).

Perhaps you have different drivers than the ones listed below. If so, add them to your worksheet and rank them along with the others. The top five are your Perseverance Drivers. These are the motivators you will draw upon most frequently when your determination starts to flag. They will help you reignite your passion and summon the will you'll need to achieve your vision of success.

"Insight Route" Worksheet—Driver Self-Assessment			
Driver	Importance	Driver	Importance
Money		Recognition/Awards	
Promotions		Sense of Accomplishment	
Reputation		Independence	
Respect		Competing and Winning	
Pride/Honor		Rising to a Challenge	

In chapter 1, we emphasized the importance of defining your Summit Goals in terms that are specific and quantifiable. Then we showed you how to write them down on your Vision, Summit, and Activities cards so you could review them daily. Now it's time to add a fourth card to the mix. This will be your **Perseverance Card**. On this card, you'll write down the Perseverance Drivers that will inspire you to achieve your vision of success. We'll illustrate this using the cards we created in chapter 1.

VISION CARD

I will:

Lead my team to top performance.

Achieve President's Club.

Be promoted to VP of sales.

Stand on the summit of Everest.

SUMMIT CARD

I will:

Blow away my $300 million goal.

Achieve my stretch goal of $400 million.

Complete a hundred hikes (2,000-vertical-foot gain each) within twelve months.

ACTIVITIES CARD

I will:

Increase my client face time.

Decrease my administrative task load.

Build stronger relationships with my clients.

Focus upon and create detailed account plans for top ten clients.

PERSEVERANCE CARD

I will:

Earn **recognition** for my leadership abilities.

Help my family achieve our financial goals.

Advance in my career.

Feel the pride of joining the elite group of Everest climbers.

Whenever you feel discouraged after a setback or can't summon the motivation to attack the high-priority items on your daily "to do" list, take a fresh look at your Vision, Summit, Activities, and Perseverance cards. Now, throttle up and get moving!

Persisting in the Face of "No"

As salespeople, we hear the word *no* much more frequently than the word *yes*. To the average performer, this can signal the end of their hopes for a sale. Deflated and discouraged, they retreat, avoiding all contact with the prospect and spiraling into self-pity. Some may even feel so defeated that they decide to leave the profession entirely. Others, made of sterner stuff, gradually summon the energy to re-engage and start prospecting again. "I gave it my best shot," they tell themselves. "It's time to move on!"

This may seem like a realistic and upbeat response to a setback. But, in fact, it's simply a way to rationalize failure and reinforce the self-defeating notion that losing is acceptable. As legendary football coach Vince Lombardi said so memorably, "Once you *learn* to quit, it becomes a habit."

Salespeople who give up this easily will never become top performers. For peak achievers, the only route to failure is quitting. Thomas Edison was undeterred by the thousands of setbacks he encountered while inventing the first commercially viable incandescent light. "I have not failed," he is quoted as saying. "I've just found ten thousand ways that won't work."

As is so often the case, Edison's apparent failures were simply the necessary prelude to his ultimate success. And each failure informed his research and helped him reach his eventual success. This is as true on the mountain as it is in business.

In chapter 1, we described how discouraged Sue felt in 2001 when she was unable to fulfill her vision of reaching the summit of Everest and how she recommitted to her goal after visiting the Olympic Training Center in Colorado Springs. It was only then that Sue fully appreciated how much she'd learned from her unsuccessful climb. She resolved to put those lessons into practice by devising a new and more rigorous training regimen.

On her next Seven Summits climb, she did a much better job of keeping herself hydrated. She stashed candy bars in the pockets of her down coat for easy access when she needed an energy boost. When Sue and Phil returned to Everest in 2002, they climbed above High Camp wearing clear goggles to ensure that their eyes would not freeze, as Phil's had the previous year. By learning from such setbacks, they created the conditions for their ultimate success.

In sales, too, coming up short is sometimes a natural and inevitable part of the process, especially when we enter new markets. But once we make that all-important first sale, we can apply what we've learned to every subsequent opportunity. We become more efficient and adept at offering industry-specific solutions that are perfectly tailored to each prospect's needs. If we keep at it, our initial failures fuel our subsequent successes.

High Pressure Doesn't Sell, Perseverance Does

"Whenever a prospect says no," Sue taught her sales team, "you should interpret this as 'not yet.' They're telling you to work harder to win their business." For top performers, "no" is a clarion call to persist and press on. This is a lesson that paid off handsomely when Sue decided to focus on selling data communications systems to the higher education market.

> I began by targeting the University of Washington in Seattle. One of the oldest public universities in the nation, the school serves more students—over 40,000 every year—than any other institu-

tion in the Northwest. I knew at the outset that the campaign would be a difficult one. A competitor had already established a strong foothold in the account and would be difficult to dislodge. It took months to schedule our first face-to-face meeting with the head of UW's data communications unit. When we finally met, he flatly rejected all of the network upgrade options my team and I recommended.

Undeterred, I continued to schedule follow-up meetings, where we shared information about emerging data networking technologies and described how we were helping other clients secure the best return from their network investments. Over time, our prospect came to value these sessions and began treating me as a guide, rather than as a salesperson.

Finally, thanks to our diligence in nurturing this relationship, we were able to win a small piece of business when the university opened a new off-campus facility. My team and I hastened to make the most of the opportunity, working hard to ensure that the installation went smoothly and that the client was delighted with the quality and responsiveness of our service.

Based on this success, my firm was invited to bid on a multi-million-dollar contract to design and install a very large and complex data network in Seattle. I assembled a crack account team and marshaled all of our resources to win the deal. But, once again, we came up short and the deal went to the incumbent.

Despite my keen disappointment, I resolved to soldier on. Again and again, I reassessed our strategy and tried new approaches. Finally, almost five years after our initial meeting, we won what turned out to be one of my firm's largest and most significant deals in the education market. Our dogged perseverance had transformed repeated failures into a stunning success!

Rerouting Around the "No"

When the route up a mountain becomes impassable, a guide blazes a new trail to the summit. When a sales campaign ends in temporary failure, top performers take the following critical steps to "Reroute around the 'No.'"

- **Ask Why**. This may seem obvious. But you'd be surprised how often the average performer flees the scene when they encounter the dreaded "no." It's essential that you fully understand a prospect's reasons for going with a competitor. Were there shortcomings in your proposal? Did you overlook business problems they wanted you to address or underestimate their importance? Perhaps your prospect missed some of the key benefits of your solution. Was it a pricing issue? Perhaps your pricing was competitive but presented in a way they found difficult to follow. Was the competitor's proposal truly superior? Since companies tend to lead with their strengths, competing proposals seldom allow direct apples-to-apples comparisons. Make sure your prospect fully understands how your solution stacks up against the competition. Rejection can sometimes be rapidly reversed through clarification and explanation.

- **Consult with Your Team**. You've relied on your Inside and Outside ROPE teams to provide you with constructive feedback and suggestions throughout every phase of the sales campaign. Go to them now and ask for their honest opinions about what went wrong. Don't be defensive. They're giving you the crucial information you'll need to win next time. They may even surprise you with great ideas for spotlighting the critical weaknesses of the winning proposal or cost-effective enhancements that will enable you to overcome your competitor's advantages. This may be the ammunition you need to convince the prospect to reopen the decision-making process.

- **Take a Risk**. If the deal is done, then you have nothing more to lose by taking a risk. Ask an industry expert on your Outside ROPE team to contact your prospect and argue on your behalf. Try to arrange a meeting between the leadership teams at your respective companies. Sometimes large deals can be brokered only at the highest levels. Write an e-mail to your customer expressing your intent to win them back. Show your passion!

- **Stay Positive**. Your prospect didn't set out to make you feel bad or reject you personally. Most likely, the reverse is true. They enjoyed the enthusiasm you brought to the sales campaign and appreciated your commitment to helping them succeed. Now it's time to build on this goodwill. Be gracious. Demonstrate your intention to continue seeking creative, cost-effective solutions to their business problems. They'll appreciate your candor and respect your professionalism. "No" can be the springboard to deeper, more enduring relationships.

- **Stay Engaged**. Sometimes you can lose a battle but win the war. In their zeal to win the business, your competitor may have overstated their capabilities. The low pricing they offered may now be offset by the low quality of the products and services they deliver. They may miss important deadlines that cause the prospect to lose confidence and reconsider their decision. By staying engaged as your client's guide, you maintain the open communications necessary to learn about these issues and the credibility to win back the business if the opportunity arises.

Of course, there's a big difference between persevering and being a pest. A pest keeps calling on a prospect without offering anything new. They reiterate their pet message points over and over again, re-hashing the benefits of a solution their prospect has already rejected.

Top performers behave quite differently. They return to Base Camp and update their account plans. They perform new industry research, seeking information and insights that will allow the prospect to anticipate and respond to their next set of business challenges. They reinvest in nurturing their relationships with key decision makers and influencers. In short, they serve as a guide, always keeping their prospect's interests in mind and continually searching for new ways to achieve mutual success.

Perseverance and Leadership

In *Man and Superman,* George Bernard Shaw famously wrote, "He who can, does. He who cannot, teaches." But when it comes to sales, nothing could be further from the truth.

Thanks to their ability to close business, top performers are often promoted into positions of great authority. Many of our nation's most successful companies are headed by CEOs who began their careers in sales and then rose steadily through the ranks.

Sales executives take on a new challenge when they step into management. They must now help their team members develop the same knowledge and skills they acquired on their long and arduous climb to the summit of sales success. They must apply the principles of becoming a guide to inspire the next generation of top performers. In short, they must:

- **Mentor and Teach**. As a sales rep, your primary goal was to meet your individual sales quota. Now you're responsible for an entire sales team that's charged with producing a significant portion of your company's revenue. Effective leaders draw on their experience to motivate and guide others. They are empathetic and supportive, encouraging their team members and empowering them to achieve their full potential.

- **Set High Expectations**. Sales leaders know that it's all too easy to live down to low expectations. So they set ambitious goals for each team member and express unshakable faith in their ability to excel. In response to setbacks, leaders offer constructive feedback and advice. They never embarrass their direct reports by criticizing them in public or try to motivate them through intimidation.

- **Build Trust**. Strong leaders treat their teams with respect. They build trust by listening carefully to each individual's concerns and consistently following through on their commitments. They're also willing to offer a helping hand from time to time when a team member feels overwhelmed or overburdened.

- **Provide Recognition**. Everyone thrives on recognition. When a team member meets a goal, be sure to congratulate them both individually and in a group setting. This has multiple benefits. First, they'll feel freshly motivated to pursue their next goal. Secondly, it will inspire their fellow team members to redouble their efforts to win similar recognition.

- **Celebrate Your Team's Achievements**. Make sure the leaders of your company know about the contributions made by everyone on your sales and Inside ROPE teams in closing an important piece of business or achieving some other important goal. Take your team off-site at least once a month to celebrate each of their contributions and to recharge everyone's commitments. Employees are most loyal and productive when they feel appreciated and engaged.

- **Climb Higher**. Never allow yourself or your team to become over-confident or complacent. Climbers know from hard experience that the summit is not the finish line. The elation of reaching the summit and the exhaustion from the supreme effort to arrive there can lead climbers to make critical—sometimes fatal—mistakes when they descend. On the mountain, *complacency can get you killed!* The same is true in sales, where *complacency can get you fired!* Continue challenging yourself and your team to set and achieve ambitious goals. Conceive a new and even more compelling vision of success. Keep climbing higher!

There's No Greater High Than Achieving Your Dream

On March 20, 2002, Sue sat in her office checking her e-mail for the last time, thinking about the challenges ahead. Ten months had passed since she and Phil had been forced to defer their shared Everest dream and turn back, only 1,400 feet from the summit. Today they would return to Nepal and begin their second attempt to reach the summit together. Since she resolved to return to Everest, Sue hadn't allowed herself to consider the possibility of a second failure. But suddenly, she was besieged by doubts. As she recalls:

> In 2002, the odds for a couple to succeed on Everest were a scant one in ten. For the past two years, I had been pursuing a goal with a 90 percent failure rate. Was I overreaching, committing myself to a lost cause that might cost both of us our lives?
>
> Just then my computer chimed, indicating that a new e-mail had arrived in my in-box. It was a "quote of the day" message by GM founder William C. Durant that read, "Forget past mistakes. Forget failures. Forget everything except what you're going

to do now and do it." I printed out the quote, placed it in my backpack, and headed for the airport.

The next two months would test my ability to persevere as never before. I would endure oxygen deprivation, headaches, insomnia, and extreme nausea. I would grieve when climber Peter Legate fell to his death descending the Lhotse Face. I would read and reread the Durant quote whenever I needed fresh resolve to face the day ahead.

After eight challenging weeks on Everest, Phil and I passed the Balcony, the landmark at 27,600 feet where we had been forced to turn back the year before. As we neared the South Summit, Phil pulled down his oxygen mask, leaned in close to my ear, and said, "Sue, this is a once-in-a-lifetime opportunity. Take it in. Burn all of this into your mind."

All of us have moments in our lives that we cherish above all others. This was one of those for me. I have never forgotten the thrill I felt as Phil and I stood at the summit, surrounded by the jagged-edged peaks of the mighty Himalayas rising into the cloudless blue sky.

On May 16, 2002, Phil and I took the final step of a ten-year journey that had taken me from novice climber to the summit of Everest. We became the first couple in history to climb the Seven Summits. Gazing out at the endless vista with Phil at my side, I felt an extraordinary sense of contentment. I had achieved all of my goals—first in business and now in my personal life. At age forty-six, my life seemed complete.

Sue and John were driven by a fierce desire to join the elite club of roughly 1,300 climbers who had successfully summited Everest by 2001. One of their rewards for achieving this coveted goal was waiting for them in Kathmandu.

The Rum Doodle Bar & Restaurant is named after *The Ascent of Rum Doodle*, a comic novel written by W. E. Bowman in 1956.

The story centers on a team of hapless Englishmen attempting to climb the fictional Mount Doodle which, at 40,000 and one-half feet, would be the tallest in the world, if it existed.

Climbers who successfully summit Everest are granted two special privileges at the Rum Doodle. First, they're allowed to eat and drink there free of charge for the rest of their lives. Second, and most importantly, they earn the privilege of writing their name on the wooden boards mounted behind the bar, joining such climbing greats as Sir Edmund Hillary, Tenzing Norgay, Jim Whittaker, and Phil Ershler!

> On the eve of her second attempt to summit Everest, Sue sat at the Rum Doodle bar with her husband, Phil, and their friend and guide, Mark. Although Mark had successfully climbed Everest in 1990, he had never claimed the Rum Doodle recognition that was his rightful due.
>
> Sue watched as the bartender handed Mark a black felt marker and pointed to an open spot on the board. After Mark signed his name, the bartender rang a bell and everyone at the bar broke into loud applause. Sue recalls vividly what happened next:
>
> As the crowd congratulated Mark for his Everest achievement, I felt a surge of confidence and determination. Mark had proven that my vision to reach the summit was within my grasp if I was willing to persevere. At that moment, I resolved to return to the Rum Doodle and add my name to the hallowed board of Everest summiteers.
>
> Two months later, I made good on this commitment and returned with Phil to the Rum Doodle, so excited I could barely touch the first real meal I'd enjoyed since our arrival at Everest Base Camp. Afterward, we went behind the bar and signed our names. Just as I had imagined, the bartender rang the bell and the climbers crowding the restaurant roared their approval.

Sue signing her name at the Rum Doodle. *(Phil Ershler)*

*Someone placed drinks in our hands and we toasted each other.
I felt a deep sense of gratitude and contentment. I had achieved
my vision.*

*Today, when people ask me why I climbed Everest, I simply
tell them, "The Rum Doodle!"*

You too can experience the tremendous sense of closure and satisfaction that comes with overcoming your perceived limitations and
achieving something real and meaningful.

What does *your* board look like? Are you ready to muster the perseverance you'll need to earn the right to make *your* mark? If you do,
you'll experience something profound and life changing. Whenever
you encounter disappointments or setbacks, you'll be able to call on
this memory of sublime achievement and feel reinvigorated. You'll
gain a Perseverance Driver that will sustain you throughout your
career and beyond. Remember:

✓ Perseverance is a **skill** you can develop and strengthen through **practice**.

✓ Identify and harness your **Perseverance Drivers** by traversing the Insight Route.

✓ High pressure doesn't sell, **perseverance** does.

✓ When you hear "No," it only means, **"Not yet!"**

✓ Your Inside and Outside Route teams can help you **"Reroute around the 'No.'"**

✓ You only **fail** when you **stop trying**.

✓ Surround yourself with people who **won't let you quit**.

✓ Top performers know that pain is temporary but **pride is forever**.

We hope you found this book both informative and inspiring. It took us decades to acquire and learn to consistently apply the skills and attitudes shared by top performers on the mountain and in business. If you persevere in putting our lessons into practice, you'll reach new peaks of performance that you never dreamed were possible. Nothing will hold you back from achieving your most cherished visions of success.

As sales leaders, Sue and John have won numerous rewards and recognition for their achievements. During her twenty-three-year corporate career, Sue held a series of increasingly responsible executive positions in the sales divisions of Fortune 500 companies, including Verizon, Qwest, United Technologies, and FedEx. She consistently led her teams to numerous sales records, beating objectives from $1 million to $600 million, ultimately as a vice president. Today she is a renowned keynote speaker, traveling the world sharing her expertise and experiences with executives and their teams at leading corporations.

After a successful beginning in sales at the Xerox Corporation, John was recruited by Verizon to form their data and video communications business, where he became a top national sales performer. John later served as vice president of marketing and operations for Northland Communications Corporation, a national provider of cable and Internet services. He subsequently launched a boutique investment banking firm and served as CEO of Saltmine Inc., a Seattle-based software company. John is currently managing director and partner at Delafield Hambrecht, Inc. (DHI), a merchant bank headquartered in Seattle. DHI is a registered investment advisor that manages hedge funds and makes private equity investments.

> *If you can't fly, run. If you can't run, walk. If you can't walk, crawl. But by all means, keep moving.*
>
> —*Martin Luther King Jr.*

John reaches the summit of Mount
Everest—May 26, 2001.

Sue and Phil reach the summit of Mount
Everest—May 16, 2002.

AUTHORS' NOTE

Despite their busy careers, Sue and John still find time to challenge themselves by testing their physical limits. John is a dedicated runner who has successfully completed eleven marathons. He also enjoys skiing, biking, yachting, and golf. In 2012, Sue completed her third successful climb of Mount Kilimanjaro. She has climbed mountains with an average elevation of more than 16,000 feet more than fifty times. She also works out almost every day and enjoys hiking, bodybuilding, skiing, and paddleboarding and other water sports.

PROFILES IN PERSEVERANCE

No major achievement is ever won easily. You need vision, a plan, and the dogged perseverance to carry it through. You must find the fortitude to overcome every obstacle in your path—refusing to give up, fighting every step of the way until you achieve your dream. We hope the following Profiles in Perseverance will inspire you to follow the example of these two highly successful business leaders.

JOHN S. WHETZELL

Chief Executive Officer and Director, Northland Telecommunications Corporation

John served as chief executive officer of Northland Cable Television Inc. since Februrary 1982 and as chief executive officer and chairman since December 1984. He is also the founder of Northland Communications Corporation, which owns and operates cable television systems in eight states. Whetzell has been involved with the cable television industry for more than forty years, beginning with a stint as chief economist of the Cable Television Bureau of the Federal Communications Commission (FCC) from May 1974 to February 1979.

He left the FCC to lead the national cable television services consulting practice for Ernst & Whinney (now EY), a post he held until February 1982, when he decided to found his own cable television business. He holds an undergraduate degree in economics from George Washington University and earned his MBA from New York University.

"In March 1981, the Federal Reserve Bank started taking drastic steps to lead the nation out of a decade of stagflation. Soon, policies led to 16 percent prime rate and inflation reaching over 13 percent. You could hardly have chosen a worse time to start a new business. Still, after two years as a consultant with Ernst & Whinney and a stint with the Federal Communications Commission, I felt I could no longer defer my dream to launch a cable television company of my own.

At the time, most small towns received cable service from a single provider. Many of these companies provided poor service and operated inefficiently because they had no competitors. This was unlikely to change, given the huge investment capital required to build out a new cable television infrastructure, especially now that interest rates were so exorbitant. But I had detected a financing opportunity I felt was too good to pass up. I was convinced that I could raise the capital I needed by forming limited partnerships with groups of investors, who would appreciate the tax shelter this provided as much as the potential for extremely favorable returns.

When I started sharing my ideas with friends and acquaintances, the feedback was anything but encouraging. The reactions ranged from lukewarm to frankly incredulous. "You've never operated a cable company and you have no experience in raising capital," many pointed out. But they failed to dissuade me. Instead I focused on finding people who could serve as guides and allies in helping me achieve my vision. My first break came when an insurance executive I met on a plane mentioned that his firm was actively engaged in raising capital for limited partnerships. I asked for his card and arranged a meeting with him soon afterward.

At the meeting, he was cordial but little more. He asked to see my business plan, which, of course, I didn't have. At first I thought this might simply be his way of dismissing me. But then I decided to treat his challenge as an opportunity.

Enlisting the help of several colleagues, I took a week off from work and labored day and night writing what I felt was a comprehensive and convincing business case. After reviewing it, the insurance executive was sufficiently impressed to introduce me to several of his former fraternity brothers, who practiced business law. They agreed to take the risk of providing me with legal services in exchange for a promise to pay their fees and grant them a small portion of company stock, should we secure funding.

Every hurdle I overcame was followed by another seemingly insurmountable one. A group of potential investors demanded answers to three key questions: (1) Where would I find an existing cable system to purchase at a price that offered sufficient upside to investors? (2) How would I leverage the purchase without a bank loan? and (3) Where would I find brokers to sell the limited partnership interests? It quickly became apparent that I would need to have a deal in place before I could start raising capital. Somehow I would have to convince the seller that I had sufficient funds to make a purchase while asking them to finance at least part of the purchase price. So my next challenge was finding a broker to help me locate a suitable cable system.

After months of effort, I finally found a broker willing to work with me. Together we found a small cable system in Oakhurst, California, near Yosemite National Park, which was proving difficult for the brokerage to sell because the owner was demanding such a high price. However, on the positive side, the system was generating a significant cash flow and the town's location was highly desirable. I concluded that the price was reasonable. I also began bidding on building a new cable franchise for the city of Woodburn, Oregon, which I knew to be an extreme long shot. Still, I persisted; driving six hours round-trip several times a week to meet with Woodburn's mayor and other community leaders.

The next hurdle was locating financial brokers who would sell limited partnership interests. The insurance executive, who by now was astounded by my nerve, suggested that I hire a consultant. I did so and off we proceeded to find a willing and well-connected broker.

This too proved to be extremely difficult and discouraging. At any given time, one or more critical parts of the deal threatened to go south. I only got through the ups and downs by having a fearless and mindless perseverance. I simply refused to give up.

Before the ordeal was over, I had taken out a second mortgage on my home and faced severe financial difficulties. Finally, on June 30, 1982, we managed to successfully fund the limited partnership and won the franchise to build the Woodburn system. However, we knew that we needed to put together at least four more partnerships over the next year to gain enough revenue to subsist in the long run as a viable company. We accomplished this goal, and the rest is history.

Once it worked out, our gratitude at having the opportunity to fulfill our dream kept all of us involved and motivated to succeed through many trials and tribulations that would face us as well as the industry. Looking back, I remember the words of one entrepreneur who, when asked how he did it, responded, "I was just too dumb to know I couldn't do it!"

JOHN WOJICK

Senior Vice President, Global Sales for Boeing Commercial Airplanes

John Wojick is responsible for the sales of Boeing's commercial airplanes and related services to airlines and leasing customers in all markets worldwide. He has held several high-level positions within the sales organization since 2002. He previously served as the vice president for North America Sales, which he assumed in February 2012. Prior to leading North America Sales, Wojick was the vice president of Asia Pacific and India Sales.

From October 2008 until 2010, Wojick served as vice president of sales for Leasing and Asset Management, Commercial Airplanes. He also was responsible for Boeing Business Jets. From 2002 to 2008, he was vice president of sales for Latin America and the Caribbean.

Previously, Wojick had served as a commercial airplanes sales director and was responsible for Continental Airlines, Federal Express, National, and several other U.S. airlines. From 1994 to 1996, he led sales for used and VIP airplanes and was involved in the discussions that led to the launch of Boeing Business Jets.

Wojick joined Boeing in 1980 as an aerospace engineer and held a number of assignments in maintenance and systems training, flight operations engineering, internal audit, and marketing. He graduated with honors from the University of Colorado in 1980 with a bachelor of science in aerospace engineering and earned his master of business administration from the University of Colorado in 1985.

"In the first two weeks of January 2013, two battery failure incidents on the Boeing 787 led to the FAA grounding the entire fleet. This was the first time an airplane fleet had been grounded by the FAA in over thirty years. Boeing only had fifty of these airplanes delivered at the time and initially it was unclear what was going to be required to get the 787 back in service.

With more than nine hundred aircraft on order with more than fifty-seven customers, we worked diligently to assure them that we would minimize disruption to their fleet plans. Over the following three months, many hundreds of Boeing employees put in an all-out effort to design, test, certify, build, and install a solution that enhanced the battery system and got us back in the air.

During this time period, my sales team and I diligently and continuously communicated with all our customers to ensure they understood the situation and the efforts that Boeing was exerting to rectify the situation. It took amazing perseverance and skill for the Boeing team to develop and execute a plan and solution that would have taken a lesser team years to implement. At the same time we worked to demonstrate to our customers that Boeing deserved their trust and would rectify this situation safely and efficiently.

On April 27, the first 787 returned to service. We kept all of our customers; nobody canceled an order, and all of our customers stayed with their commitments to the 787.

By persevering and staying close to our customers during extremely trying and difficult times, we have built relationships that will last for decades."

JOHN MEISENBACH

Founder and Chairman, MCM

John Meisenbach is the founder and chairman of MCM, an employee benefits and insurance brokerage business he created in Seattle, Washington. After serving in the United States Navy Submarine Service, John graduated from Seattle University and soon launched MCM in 1962. Through John's drive, determination, and perseverance, MCM would grow over the next five decades to become one of the largest privately held companies in the Northwest. His insurance brokerage business alone attained premium volume of $988.7 million in 2013. MCM currently holds awards for *Seattle Business* magazine's Washington's 100 Best Companies to Work For, as well as the *Puget Sound Business Journal*'s Washington's Best Workplaces, Washington's Top 75 Corporate Philanthropists, and Washington's Top Insurance Brokerages.

Beyond his success in the financial services industry, John's vision and support helped several other businesses, notably Costco Wholesale. Beyond serving on the board of Costco, John also serves on the boards of Expeditor's International, M Financial Group, Children's Hospital Foundation, and America's Foundation for Chess.

Additionally, he is committed to his community and supports several organizations, including United Way of King County, Global Partnerships, Medical Teams International, Atlantic Street Center, Zion Preparatory Academy, and Seattle University.

> Perseverance is the ability to keep moving forward when most would yield to obstacles and objections. I started MCM in my twenties, and there were plenty of obstacles in the benefits and insurance industry. I simply vowed to outwork my competition. I set a goal of meeting with four to five people every day, both prospects and customers. That was in addition to working with a growing number of employees and strategic partners. I still try to meet that standard today. I told my sales teams routinely: If you aren't having breakfast and lunch with a prospect or a customer, don't eat. When perseverance and vision meet, great things can happen.

AFTERWORD

If you're ever fortunate enough to visit Nepal, you'll never forget your first sight of the mighty Himalayas as they tower, otherworldly and serene, into the farthest reaches of the sky. You'll also come to respect the dignity, resilience, and proud culture of the Nepali people who call this wondrous land their home. Sadly, Nepal remains one of the poorest countries in the world. Many homes lack electricity and plumbing, forcing family members to fetch and carry water in containers on their backs. The Nepali must often cook their meals over wood fires and burn yak dung in stoves to heat their homes. It's a hard life.

Women, especially, are at risk. Today Nepal has one of the lowest female literacy rates in the world. According to the American Himalayan Foundation (AHF), a nonprofit organization dedicated to supporting education, health care, and cultural and environmental preservation throughout the Himalayan region, "Every year, as many as twenty thousand young girls from the poorest parts of Nepal are trafficked into brothels or domestic servitude from as far away as the Middle East."

Sue and John are proud to partner with the American Himalayan Foundation by donating a portion of the proceeds from this book to AHF's "Stop Girl Trafficking" project, which has helped thousands of Nepali girls stay in school and become valued members of their communities. If you'd like to learn more about the AHF and its programs, please visit http://susanershler.com/community.html.

APPENDIX

FROM EVEREST TO THE EXECUTIVE SUITE: THREE TIPS FOR ASPIRING C-LEVEL EXECUTIVES
(*This article was originally published in* Forbes Woman *magazine.*)

In my career as a Fortune 500 sales executive and a Seven Summits mountain climber, I've developed a set of guiding principles that have allowed me to achieve seemingly impossible revenue goals while simultaneously climbing the world's highest mountains. Yet I don't consider myself to be exceptionally gifted or unique. Anyone who is prepared to commit the time and effort can be equally successful if they Project · Prepare · Persevere®. These are the by-words to a systematic approach I've developed for achieving what some might consider to be unachievable goals.

To illustrate this, here are three lessons I learned from my most difficult and exhilarating climbs:

PROJECT
Lesson: Every success begins with an ambitious and clearly articulated vision. It's essential to project your future and clearly define a vision for yourself and your team.

During my year of intense physical training for Everest, I visualized myself and my husband, Phil, standing together, triumphant at the summit. It was an image I would revisit many times every day until it was so vivid and real, I could almost reach out and touch the snowy peaks and breathe the thin, frigid air. In 2002, my vision was realized when Phil and I stood atop Everest's highest peak, becoming the first couple in history to scale the Seven Summits.

I took exactly the same approach as a sales leader, consistently setting seemingly impossible goals and then surrounding myself with images that, to me, constituted success. For example, I would place placards showing my team's revenue objectives throughout my office and visualize our CEO congratulating us on having exceeded our numbers. After several months of this sustained visualization, I found myself gradually changing my viewpoint about my goal. What was once unthinkable became not only possible, but excitingly within reach. In my view, an extravagant goal both focuses and energizes you, simultaneously expanding your sense of your own capabilities and of life's possibilities.

PREPARE

Lesson: No mountain is scaled in a single climb, no quota achieved in a single day. You must create a detailed road map that delineates every step of your journey and includes tangible benchmarks to measure success along the way.

I had been climbing for only two years when Phil and I set out to ascend Mount McKinley, the highest peak in North America, which stands over 20,000 feet. The day was clear and cold when our small plane touched its skis down on the ice-covered landing strip. Towering ahead of us, I could see the massive bulk of McKinley. I fell in behind the other climbers, carrying a very heavy pack and pulling a sled weighted down with gear. The air was so thin I could barely breathe. As we approached a deadly crevasse field, I found myself gasping for air and thinking, "This is ridiculous. I'm nowhere near ready for this type of expedition. If it's so difficult now, I'll never make it to the top. I shouldn't even be here."

With every self-defeating thought, I slowed until I was down to a snail's pace, fighting back tears. As the only female, I was determined not to show weakness. Fortunately Phil noticed and walked back to steady me. "Relax," he told me. "We're not going to climb the whole mountain today. We'll go up in stages, from one camp to the next. In a few weeks, with luck and good weather, we'll have one day left and that will be the day we reach the summit. Just like 'eating an elephant,' you do it one bite at a time."

From then on, I concentrated on reaching the next camp. When that no longer worked, I persevered in making it to the next rest break. When that became too much, I focused on picking up each leg and then stepping forward. In the end, we stood together on the summit, just as I'd imagined.

Phil's advice applies equally well to achieving any business objective. As a leader, you have to create a detailed road map that breaks even the most daunting goal down into manageable steps, with tangible benchmarks for success along the way. As a senior sales executive, I helped my team prepare for success by creating activity, territory, and account plans that generated $600 million in annual revenue, exceeding our quotas 120 to 200 percent for thirteen out of fifteen years.

PERSEVERE

Lesson: All great achievements are realized by committing to a goal and then working ceaselessly to attain it.

After sixty-three days of climbing Everest, Phil and I had just one day left to make it to the top. We began our final ascent at two-thirty in the morning, struggling against the bitter cold and heavy winds blowing snow horizontally into our faces. When we were just 1,400 feet from the summit—an elevation of about 27,600 feet—we stopped on an icy ledge to change our oxygen bottles. Lightning strikes in the distance would briefly pierce the gloom with an unearthly light.

After assessing the conditions, Phil turned to me, shouting to be heard over the howling of the wind. "I can't take you up in this storm. We need to go down, can you live with that?" At first, I felt a great relief, simply grateful to be alive. But as we began our descent, I suddenly understood the climb was truly over. After sixty days of tough climbing, two years of relentless training and putting my personal life on hold, my dream of standing atop Everest would not be fulfilled that day.

As we began heading down the mountain, I saw Phil stumbling, something he had never done during any of our prior climbs. This worsened as we continued our descent. Finally, he turned to me and asked if there was something wrong with his eyes. I saw that there were small icicles hanging from his eyebrows and lashes. But when I peered closer, I realized that his brown eyes had turned a purplish hue. His eyes had frozen over! He later told me it felt like he was trying to see through waxed paper. Thank goodness we had turned around. Phil might have lost his vision entirely or suffered a fatal accident. It had been the right decision to stop, even though we were so close to reaching our goal.

A year later, we returned to Everest and reached the summit. It was a moment I will never forget, a dream finally fulfilled.

This kind of perseverance is equally important in business. I'm a strong believer in the value of hard work, dedication, and disciplined teamwork within an organization. I taught my sales team to take every "No" as a "Not Yet," to understand every rejection as a challenge to improve, innovate, and persevere. And then, like ascending Everest, to return again and again until the account was won and the sale closed. In business, as in life, if you persevere and stay focused, you will wake up one day and find yourself having achieved your loftiest ambition. When you do, it will be time to project your next achievement and begin the whole amazing process once again.

VIEW FROM THE TOP:
AN ALUMNI PROFILE OF JOHN WAECHTER
This article was originally published in the Fall 2001 issue of UW Business *from the Foster Business School.*

Since creatures resembling ourselves began roaming the earth some 100,000 years ago, only fifty-four *Homo sapiens* have stood atop the highest point on all seven continents. While the "Seven Summits

Club" is among the most exclusive on the planet, it's also among the most democratic: open to anyone with the skill, stamina, and courage to climb more than twelve vertical miles over rock, snow, and ice—amid raging winds, numbing cold, and thin, comfortless air.

On May 25 of this year, John Waechter (MBA 1995), earned entry into this elite fraternity by climbing the last and most difficult of the seven summits, Mount Everest. "When you get to the top of Everest, it's very different from any other mountain I've climbed," John says. "You may be standing on top of the world, but there is no sense of triumph or exhilaration. Because you know the job is only half-done. You still have to get back down."

Most mountaineering accidents occur on the descent, particularly on 8,000-meter peaks like Everest, where exhaustion can lead to a fatal misstep, and killing storms can move in quickly, trapping climbers at high altitude. Although Waechter got down safely, taking about eight hours to negotiate 3,000 vertical feet, he did come perilously close to that end stage of exhaustion at high altitude when some climbers simply sit down and never get up. "Because our water bottles had frozen," he recalls, "I was exhausted on the descent and dangerously dehydrated—having taken in only a few ounces of liquid in more than sixteen hours of climbing."

Fortunately John had squirreled away some tea in a small thermos—which didn't freeze. "When we finally stopped to rest and I drank the last of that precious tea, I got a mental boost—and I knew I was going to make it back."

Seeing things through to the finish, and planning ahead wisely to get the job done, are two of the trademarks of John Waechter's life and career. After graduating from Whitman College in 1984, he started his business career in sales at Xerox, before moving on to GTE Northwest in a senior marketing position, and returning to University of Washington Business School to get his MBA. An avid marathoner and mountaineer, John climbed Mount Kilimanjaro in 1994 with the legendary Dick Bass—the first man to complete the

Seven Summits. Dick inspired John to pursue his quest, which took seven years and involved expeditions to some of the most remote, inhospitable regions on earth—including the interior of Antarctica.

Now that he's achieved his mountaineering dream, Waechter, at age thirty-nine, is channeling his energy into building the business he cofounded in 1997, Waechter Lufkin, LLC. "No," he confirms, "climbing Everest is not particularly good for business. Try coming home to two months of unanswered phone messages and accumulated e-mail!"

Waechter Lufkin raises private equity for emerging growth companies. John loves the challenge of working with technology start-ups in their efforts to create successful enterprises. It's a fast-paced, high-risk, high-reward form of consulting that's suited to his personality.

Having been to the top of the world, does Waechter feel that ordinary life is a bit tame by comparison? "You don't compare," he says. "You apply what you've learned to the task at hand."

That's a trait that has gotten John Waechter from the classroom to the boardroom to the unforgiving slopes of Everest, and back.

ABOUT THE AUTHORS

Susan Ershler and her husband, Phil, became the first couple in history to climb the Seven Summits. She is an international speaker and award-winning executive who has served in leadership positions for Fortune 500 companies for more than two decades. She is the author of *Together on Top of the World*. Visit Sue online at www .SusanErshler.com.

John Waechter serves as managing director and partner at Delafield Hambrecht, an investment firm in Seattle. He began his career in sales with the Xerox Corporation and GTE (Verizon). He has held senior management positions at Northland Communications and was CEO of Saltmine, John has also climbed the Seven Summits. Visit John online at www.7summitsinstitute.com.